back
HOME

back HOME

how the world watched
France 98

First published in 1998 by WSC Books Ltd
9 Whitehall Park, London N19 3TS

ISBN 1 897850 73 5
Printed in the UK by Biddles, Guildford

Edited by Andy Lyons and Mike Ticher
Design by Doug Cheeseman
Cover Illustration by Mick Marston
Translations by Richard Guy

CONTENTS

INTRODUCTION

There were at least two

World Cups going on in June and July 1998. One, increasingly popular in the media and sometimes in reality, was a vast international shirt-swapping fest, a chance to get blind drunk with like-minded people from faraway places and cement the undying emotional bonds between the people of Scotland and Romania, or wherever.

The other was an unattractive outpouring of nationalist fervour, which swept along millions of people who neither know nor care about football in the desire to see their country's representatives wipe the floor with treacherous neighbours/economic oppressors/ uncivilised savages (delete as appropriate). The widespread ill-feeling so easily stirred up by international football cannot be wished away no matter how many smiling children FIFA dragoon into their multicultural pageants.

Neither account, of course, is wholly true, or wholly false. But what is almost entirely lacking in both is any genuine interest in the way football is experienced in other countries. Foreign countries, for all the influence of imports in the British game, are still seen to a large extent as too exotic to be taken seriously in the press. Despite recent improvements, coverage tends to revolve around eccentric individuals and wacky incidents that reinforce the impression that foreign football is only interesting when it's crazy.

Back Home is an attempt to catch a glimpse of the 1998 World Cup as it really happened around the world, beyond the images of

7

opposing fans hugging or throwing bottles at each other, and beyond the commentators' cliches of happy-go-lucky Africans, dour east Europeans and samba-crazy Brazilians.

If the book has a loose theme it is one of national identity (don't worry, there are some jokes too). And France 98 may prove to be the last World Cup which lends itself to this kind of study in quite the same way. For the 2002 tournament the European television rights have been awarded not to the European Broadcasting Union, but to Germany's Kirch group, which is expected to sell them on to the highest bidder – meaning, more than likely, that European viewers may watch at least some of the matches from Japan and South Korea via BSkyB, Canal+ and other pay TV networks.

So the last World Cup of the century, and the last of the Havelange era, may also prove to have been the last to be enjoyed in full on free-to-air television in some countries – perhaps even in Britain, despite government promises to the contrary. If so, it may change the character of future tournaments significantly. For the World Cup, far more than the Premiership or the domestic league of any other country, is a magnet not just for diehard fans, but also for millions who otherwise pay little attention to the game.

The reason is obvious. The World Cup is about nations, and as the historian Eric Hobsbawm once pointed out, there are few more concrete expressions of a nation than 11 men wearing its colours on a football field. Never have we been closer to the phenomenon of entire nations sitting in front of the television screen, suffering with the fate of their footballers, than at France 98. That kind of experience changes nations as well as holding up a mirror to their weaknesses and prejudices. Which is why the events on the field or around the stadiums in France are only part of the World Cup story. Less obvious, but sometimes more interesting, is what went on back home.

Andy Lyons and Mike Ticher

ACKNOWLEDGMENTS

Sharp-witted readers

will have already noticed that although there were 32 countries competing at France 98, only 25 of them are covered in *Back Home*. That isn't because we found Paraguay or South Korea less interesting than anywhere else, but simply that, despite our best efforts, we were unable to secure the right contributions from those seven missing countries.

Inevitably in a book of this kind there are occasions where we have lapsed into foreign languages. While we have taken every care to get things right, there may be instances where we have made fools of ourselves to the entire population of South America (for example). Apologies too to accent fetishists, who may be driven to distraction.

The contributors to the book come from a wide variety of backgrounds. A few are professional writers, most have contributed to *When Saturday Comes*, but one or two had never done anything like this before in their lives. As will be obvious from their biographies on page 209, English is not necessarily their first language. Thanks are due to them in particular for wrestling with repeated demands for changes, clarifications and additional information.

the sin of pride

Dave Hill

I endured a strange,

queasy feeling during England's long, slow, painfully enthralling defeat by Argentina which removed them from the World Cup. Partly, this was due to an upset stomach quite unrelated, as it happens, to big-match nerves. But the fever and disorientation generated by my unhappy innards did not account for the emotional turbulence. There was no mistaking it: the bizarre, unnatural sensation of taking pride in my national team. Doctor, doctor, I rooted for England. Will I ever sneer again?

Wanting England to win is an ailment I have contracted remarkably little since my first and most intense experience of it in 1966 when I was eight years old and, like many boys at that age (including the young Glenn Hoddle), susceptible to what is essentially a delusional condition born of the belief that "we" are the greatest. Some grow out of it naturally – when they discover international socialism or mind-expanding drugs, for example – but others are left damaged for life (hello again, Glenn).

back
HOME

I suppose I've been lucky. In 1970 I felt sorry for Peter Bonetti, but ended the tournament running around our garden in a Brazil replica shirt. The affliction of football patriotism was all but shed on that famous night when, by getting a draw at Wembley, Poland denied England qualification for the 1974 tournament, ended the managerial reign of Sir Alf Ramsey and provoked Brian Clough to denounce goalkeeper Jan Tomaszewksi as a clown. I asked myself: why are these silly men getting so worked up? In Africa, people are starving.

From then on my indifference matured into derision. This reached its high point when I went to the 1988 European Championships in Germany to write about the manoeuvres of our brave hooligan lads, and thoroughly enjoyed watching German snatch squads make a few English skulls even more numb down dark alleys in Stuttgart. When I later watched the England team turned over by Ireland I was struck by the similarities between our shirtless boys off the the pitch and those in white shirts on it. Both examples of English manhood were predictable, artless and basically inadequate. In other words, nothing I wanted to be associated with, never mind that I was born in the same country.

During Italia 90 my scorn reached its peak. After two weeks on the road in Italy enjoying the company of travelling fans from Colombia, Scotland, Sweden and Brazil, I returned home to watch the later stages on TV and was nearly ejected from a neighbour's house for leaping with glee each time Cameroon stuck one past Shilton. As you'll recall, two Lineker penalties got Bobby Robson's side out of jail, which left a funny taste. I don't dislike Nice Gary exactly but, you know, I wouldn't mind stealing his crisps...

I passed the Graham Taylor years in a state of delicious self-satisfaction – no need to elaborate, do I not think – and anticipated Euro 96 with a lurking fear that Terry Venables's team might do well enough to trigger the sort of bingeing boastfulness at which our media excels. These fears were realised when the *Mirror*, pathetically desperate to steal the *Sun*'s readers, anticipated the semi-final against Germany with its notorious Second World War front page "joke" featuring Paul Gascoigne and Stuart Pearce in army helmets. Previously, such behaviour would have confirmed me in my heresy. But I was already discomfited by subterranean stirrings. I'd felt tremors of enthusiasm during England's 4-1 rout of Holland – subterranean but undeniable.

Perhaps it would just pass. But then I found myself reduced to a state of hopeless partisanship by the crunch France 98 qualifier in Italy. And after Hoddle named his final 22, I caught myself hoping quite hard that a squad which contained talents as exceptional as Shearer, Campbell, Beckham and Owen – and shorn of the revolting Gazza – might produce football to make me not want to disown them. What could have brought about this startling relapse? A yearning for lost youth as I plunged into my mid-life crisis? An unexpected susceptibility to the sheer volume of hype? Probably a bit of both. But neither would have affected me nearly as strongly had it not been for the contagious enthusiasm of a boy called Frankie.

Frankie was eight years old at the start of France 98, the same age as I was during the 1966 tournament. His excited anticipation of the World Cup touched and intrigued me. Which players, incidents and matches would stick in his head and still be there 30 years on? What impressions would be made on him by the behaviour of the adults around him? And how would he manifest his adoration of the England team, the same automatic loyalty I had felt at his age? Looking back, I realise that the 1966 World Cup provided me with some of my earliest and most persuasive explanations about what kind of country England was and how the character of English people was supposed to be reflected in the honest grit and endeavour of the England football team.

Many years later, it sunk in that I and Bobby Charlton had nothing at all in common except the way we both celebrated scoring a goal by leaping up and describing a forward throwing motion with one arm while in mid-air. But at the time, the fact that I could replicate this salute perfectly every time I netted for my school team expressed my strong belief that I and Bobby shared a common cause. Would similar signs of empathy and devotion become detectable in Frankie as France 98 progressed? Such questions were inspired by more than just my unhealthy appetite for social observation. Being Frankie's dad, they were also about love.

There is a ridiculous side of me which would like to describe my France 98 as big, corny father-and-son thing, a male bonding exercise accomplished without having to travel deep into a forest and live on insects for a month. It was never going to be that way. For a start there were the very different needs of my four other children to consider: my teenage daughter Laura, who regards all sport as a form of madness; her little sister Dolores, who knows little of football yet, but whose Barbies all remind me of Graeme Souness's girlfriends; my baby son Conall who actually owns a football but is far more likely to suck the thing than kick it; and seven-year-old Nat, a quiet, enigmatic, single-minded boy who, unlike the more voluble Frankie, can take football or leave it.

It was, I think, rather typical of Nat that his World Cup turned out to be a more sophisticated cultural experience than mine or Frankie's. At his best friend Yassin's house the favoured team was Morocco, homeland of Yassin's late father. At least, it was until Morocco played Brazil, when Yassin's sympathies subtly shifted to the team that was winning – in some ways kids don't change. Here was just one example of how patriotism is rarely as straightforward as Norman Tebbit used to claim, especially not round our way.

In my patch of north-east London, footballing and locational loyalties are configured with delicious complexity. For instance, we've got a chip shop run by Turks who have sayings from the Koran blu-tacked to their wall and pictures of Princess Diana sellotaped to their till. In football terms we've got chaps who cheer for Arsenal and Ireland, Arsenal and Italy, Arsenal and Nigeria and, most conspicuously during the latter half of June, Arsenal and Jamaica.

All this reminded me of the reasons for my ambivalence about supporting England. A few flags of St George hung cheerfully from tower block windows, but most of the ones I saw were attached to the rooves of Escort vans driven by psychopaths. Then came news of the disturbances in Marseille and the front-page photos of James Shayler, a creature from an inexplicable nightmare world, representing a version of Englishness that could not be further removed from the one I inhabit, a kind of alternative England of the imagination whose contrary spirit is defined by Kenneth Williams on *Round The Horne*, the miner's strike, Johnny Rotten singing *God Save The Queen* and feeling sorry for Leyton Orient – which is as near as I can get to supporting my local team.

I might have gone off the World Cup completely at the point Shayler and fellow arseholes intervened if it hadn't been for Frankie. As far as I'm aware, the incidents themselves, the ensuing cries of "shame" and mad Alan Clark MP's remarks about how the hoolies exemplified the "English martial tradition" pretty much passed him by. For Frankie, the World Cup was about heroes, especially the Manchester United players in Hoddle's squad: Gary Neville, Teddy Sheringham, Paul Scholes and, in particular, David Beckham. (The story of how Frankie became a cockney red is extremely long and tortured, but let me just make it clear that I'm not to blame.)

To Frankie, Beckham was not the posturing poppinjay and hot head that his detractors have long depicted him as. Rather, he saw him as the Man Utd man who scored a goal from inside his own half against Wimbledon, and that was just fantastic. Similarly, the day he watched Eric Cantona filming the Nike "Parklife" commercial just down the road on Hackney Marsh was not, to him, an insight into the construction of a memorable fragment of post-modernity, it was just really, really exciting. Those of us whose appetite for the opulent cosmopolitanism of the Premier League is seriously qualified by the routine obscenity of players on a basic wage of 20 grand a week can lose sight of how utterly meaningless all that stuff is to children of Frankie's age. At eight, his passion for the game was absolutely, perfectly pure.

Frankie's unequivocal keenness and my compromised scepticism provided the backdrop against which I burst through my front door just in time to watch England open their campaign against Tunisia. I had to be back from a meeting elsewhere in town in time for the one o'clock kick-off not only for selfish reasons, but also in order to tape the proceedings for Frankie who was in school. The idea was to collect him shortly after the final whistle and whisk him home to watch the recording before he could find out the result. But even as I stood in the playground at 3.30 waiting for him to emerge other kids were loudly swapping the key match details: two-nil, Shearer, Scholes. One of the teachers had had the television on in the corner of the classroom, and by the time Frankie was by my side he was already in possession of the facts. Excitement for him. Disappointment for daft dad.

We were luckier with the timing of the Romania match the following Monday, watching it together and witnessing the first appearance of Beckham, who came on as substitute following his exclusion from the first two starting line-ups. An emotional press conference performance by the Brylcreem Boy had been mocked by some as whingeing, but praised by others for its candour, and was probably interpreted by Posh Spice as proof that Beckham really is, as she has reportedly put it, "very sweet and spiritual".

Indeed, a degree of sweet spirituality had begun seeping from several parts of the England camp. Tony Adams was heard revealing how he and fellow recovering addict Paul Merson sometimes got together for heart to hearts in the absence of their usual emotional pillars – I'll bet they didn't miss Gascoigne, whose last (unintended) public appearance before being dumped by Hod took place on a golf course where he was seen rolling around on the ground with a can in his chubby hand.

The Romania game was significant for the first contributions to England's campaign by Michael Owen on the pitch and Kevin Keegan on the ITV gantry. I will not labour the contrast between the performance of the new Liverpool Mighty Mouse and the old one, now wearing a pundit's hat, and I should emphasise that I take no pleasure in adding to the avalanche of criticism aimed at Keegan who was a marvellous player, a wonderfully romantic manager of Newcastle, and is, by all accounts, a decent human being. But he is the Dan Quayle of expert analysis.

Owen, by contrast, quickly became the Boy Messiah of English football thanks to his equalising goal. And, in fact, his poacher's strike was rendered no less important by Petrescu's late winner which so embarrassed Graeme Le Saux. Frankie got over the reverse quickly, filled in his wallchart and went to bed. If this was a sign of confidence, it was justified by Beckham's dream of a free kick which finished off Colombia after Anderton's impressive opener.

Frankie and I were apart for this match. He, Nat and Laura spend half their time at the home of their mother, whom I split up with six years ago, so I can only imagine his leap of delight when his hero's curler bulged the net. I was quite pleased, however, not to have to explain the tasteful little demonstration of the joy of penetration with which Beckham celebrated. The facts of life are one thing, the metaphorical parallels between intercourse and goalscoring present a more demanding challenge altogether.

Three days before the Argentina game, the day after the victory over Colombia, Frankie had his ninth birthday – a good way of remembering the date (of the Argentina match, that is) and possibly a prescient piece of timing. Thanks to Beck, we would all be getting that ageing feeling soon enough.

Frank celebrated his big day in the only way that interested him – by playing a game of football with his schoolmates, Nat and me in the park. I love these little matches, not just because the boys present the only sort of opposition against which I can begin to emulate the command of Beckenbauer or Baresi, but because participating reminds me of the sheer pleasure of playing the game at that age. You are old enough to perform with skill, commitment and the wonderful feeling of mastery of the body, yet young enough to know nothing of the coming complications of adolescence. The boys put all the warnings about the Premier League over-heating into their proper perspective. Who cares if all the big clubs go bust tomorrow? Who cares if there is never another World Cup either? There will always be the big kick of football in the park.

Frankie was back at his mother's house as the England players prepared to face Batistuta and Ortega. I was feeling ill. Too ill to go to the boys' parents evening, and too ill to go to a school drama that Laura was appearing in (and which had been specially scheduled to enable pupils and parents alike to be back home in time for kick-off). I slumped guiltily with the baby in front of the telly, trying not to think about food or my failures as a parent. I hardly need point out that the action from St-Etienne proved a powerful distraction from guilt and the still-palpable threat of vomit. Like everyone else, I'll never forget Owen's goal, one of those moments on a football pitch when you almost can't believe what you've just seen, even after several replays. And, of course, I'll never forget the downfall of Beckham either. Or Batty and Ince missing in the penalty shoot-out. Or Owen very, very nearly doing the same.

Journalists (including me) always look for emblems in these occasions, and this one was unique for enabling the press, from the posh end of the market to the "red tops", to combine the two traditional responses to English sporting failure: heralding a glorious defeat and mercilessly punishing those responsible for it, in this case Posh Spice's unfortunate fiance. Frankie, I soon discovered, took a more measured view of his idol's fall from grace: "He was stupid, but he ought to be forgiven. Maybe in a few months' time. Do you think if I wrote to him he'd send me his autograph like Giggs did?"

As for me, the taste left by the Argentina match was unexpectedly good, and the same eventually went for the tournament itself. I loved it that France won, an imperfect collection of players who worked perfectly as a team and who, thanks to the variegated racial and cultural composition of their squad, triggered a kind of national rejoicing that completely excluded the likes of Jean-Marie Le Pen.

Actually, this aspect of the celebrations prompts an ungenerous thought about the difference between England and France as countries: you could say, chauvinistically, that, yes, some of our travelling fans act like Nazis, but at least millions of our people don't vote for them. However, both nations can – and should – argue persuasively that their football teams represented the best things about their respective homelands.

In England's case, Beckham's aberration notwithstanding, it was to do with genuine qualities which have been degraded through misuse by morons and jingoists: doggedness, pride, determination, working together against the odds in pursuit of a common goal. It will take a lot more than that to get me singing *Land Of Hope And Glory*. But I'm ready to believe there might be just a bit of truth in the old dirge after all.

national theatre

Ulrich Hesse-Lichtenberger

Act One

The zealous FIFA official walked towards the touchline and authoritatively lifted his ugly digital board, flashing a fat, red "1" to the crowd. "Oh!" blurted the German TV commentator. "Now they're taking the goalkeeper off!" Sensing that at last his time had come to report a true drama, he added breathlessly: "I haven't noticed an injury, so I can only guess at what the coach has in mind." Only then were his colleagues able to interrupt the torrent of words to remind him the game was in its dying seconds and the sign was there to tell us the referee would add on 60 seconds of stoppage time.

Such slips of either tongue or mind were commonplace in the German media coverage of France 98. There were the classic stylistic howlers ("That smacked of a hand-ball by Fish"), the awkward cliches ("The Japanese players are small but lively"), the tendency to miss crucial moments (not one journalist mentioned that Zanetti clearly handled the ball against Shearer in extra time of

Argentina v England) and the absence of tactical knowledge – both Hoddle and Passarella made one horrible, potentially fatal substitution after the other, but that was lost on the commentator because everything was so "dramatic" and "tense".

None of which is new, of course. Calling reporters incompetent and foaming at their idiosyncrasies has always been the couch potato's favourite pastime. What was peculiar about France 98, however, was that for the first ten days of the tournament the performance of the media came under just as much scrutiny as that of the players.

At one point, the director of one of the two public TV channels handling the live coverage, a political journalist by trade, was dragged in front of (his own!) cameras to counter "the public criticism of the sports commentators". Another point of debate centred around the other station's decision to hand over many of the more prestigious games to Johannes Kerner. Kerner is a jovial, rosy-cheeked youngster who is fond of trashy chat. A trained sports journalist, he cut his teeth hosting one of those confessional talk shows where hairdressers and lorry drivers harp on about marital problems.

Some thought this disqualified him for a serious sporting competition, one of them a Brazil-born colleague who in the past had handled all games involving Brazil and who couldn't understand why Kerner was chosen for the match with Holland. Incidentally, that is also why Eurosport's commercials in Germany read: "At Eurosport, the World Cup is brought to you not by a showbiz star but by a football pro – Andreas Brehme." But there were others who must have felt that nothing about this competition was really serious and that Kerner was therefore the ideal man – a man who, during Brazil v Holland, constantly referred to a football match as "a party".

France 98 was the first World Cup that really, truly, madly begged to be made into a circus by the German media. The advent of private TV in 1984 and the beginning of the football boom a few years later were the first essential ingredients, but by Italia 90 the two public channels, which still hold the rights to the European Championships and World Cup, had not yet adopted the used-car salesman's mentality that is so typical of the private stations. USA 94 was marred by the technical problem of the time difference. But even before it started, France 98 promised to have everything: a national coach who was tolerated, but not loved, taking a geriatric team and a ticking timebomb called Matthäus to meet Ronaldo & Co in a neighbouring country – on prime time.

What this meant became clear early on. The "ticket scandal" may have been a topic of great concern to fans and even politicians in other countries, but in Germany it was mainly a great media story, a tale of shady dealings and mismanagement. The reason this scandal hardly ever made it into private conversations was very simply that it held no relevance for the vast majority of German football fans – because very few of them had intended to go to France in the first place.

One reason for this has to do with the uneasiness with which Germans view displays of national pride – their own national pride, that is. Hundreds of Dutch fans decked out in orange and yelling "Hup Holland!" are regarded as colourful and enthusiastic, but the sight of a dozen Germans wrapped in their flags and chanting "Deutschland!" has an unpleasant air about it. The World Cup was less than ten days old when a regional sports weekly noticed with amazement that Germany actually had supporters. "Who are these people who are fans of the national team?" the paper asked. "Are they just regular tourists, clueless patriots from the eastern provinces or simply winners of some sort of competition?"

So the German interest in the World Cup was, as Christoph Biermann rightly noted in *When Saturday Comes*, "not intense". But he also noted it was "broad", which is equally true – if not an understatement. And that's the other reason why comparatively few Germans made the trip to France: nobody in his right mind was even thinking of missing the media spectacle at home.

There was a daily chat show on a private sports channel. Franz

Beckenbauer had his own World Cup programme for another station. The public broadcasting companies organised a travelling circus to deliver pop bands, beer and football on a giant screen to marketplaces all around the country. In almost every larger city, multiplex cinemas offered live coverage of the games. Even the church got into the act when a Catholic priest in Bavaria held a football mass ("praying for Berti", I kid you not).

The World Cup was seen not as the biggest sporting event, but as the biggest entertainment show ever. A four-week, around-the-clock, real-life soap opera. The only problem was that not too much worth reporting was happening for roughly the first two weeks. Some games were good, some were bad. But they were only games. What was lacking was a gripping, unifying, dramatic story. Which is why the media turned itself into the main story.

Act Two

I saw the first half of Germany v Yugoslavia in a *biergarten*. The man on the mike was Kerner, and he did his very best to create excitement, but the people watching were silently munching sausages and gulping beer, patiently waiting for something to happen. Only one man wore a Germany shirt, while two sported Jamaica kits. When Yugoslavia scored, the people rolled their eyes. When Matthäus warmed up, they sniggered.

For the second half, I walked over to a nearby public square where the above-mentioned travelling circus had stopped for the day. I know how this place looks when Dortmund has something to celebrate, so my guess is there were not many more than a thousand people there. Even those who had the German colours painted on their faces were staring quietly at the huge screen, trying to get drunk slowly. The only sign of any life came from a bunch of Yugoslavs waving an outsized flag.

Two hours later I was at home, just in time to catch a brief news report on how people in the same public square had seen the game.

The moment they chose was when Oliver Bierhoff scored the equaliser. The camera only caught the first few rows of faces in front of the screen, and from that you got the impression that thousands of delirious maniacs had had the day of their lives. Good cameraman. He resisted the urge to pan.

All that changed in the aftermath of the Yugoslavia game. News of how serious the riots surrounding this match had really been was slow in coming through, but once the extent was made public, anger, consternation and sorrow became more of a national topic than football or the media. The tabloids dug out all their old headlines with the word "monsters" in them, and Formula One driver Michael Schumacher got so carried away that he commented: "If these thugs were animals, one would put them to sleep."

Those of a more responsible persuasion preferred action to words and started fund-raising for Daniel Nivel, the French policeman almost beaten to death by German hooligans. From all over the country donations were sent to Nivel's family. But with hindsight, even this display of sympathy was a telling example of the lack of responsibility on the part of the DFB (the German FA) during the national team's campaign. Instead of co-ordinating the numerous, isolated efforts made by newspapers, radio stations, the German police union and countless individuals to help Nivel, the DFB went into a state of shock and did little more than hold a secret emergency meeting. It wasn't until a week after the final that the DFB finally announced they were thinking of creating a Nivel Foundation to fight football violence.

That secret meeting was a harbinger of the embarrassments to come. DFB president Edigius Braun could have held a press conference to say: "We are horrified and feel it is our moral obligation to withdraw the team, but Mr Vogts has convinced us we must not give in to brute force." Instead, it was left to the tabloids to disclose that the officials had discussed leaving the World Cup without consulting Berti Vogts, which in turn prompted Vogts to threaten he would immediately resign if the team was withdrawn.

Apparently, nobody connected to the German camp understood that at this World Cup, more than ever before, it didn't really matter what actually happened. What was important was how it appeared. And Vogts, Braun and the DFB appeared hysterical, small-minded and disorganised. Vogts especially was giving the impression he had no idea what was going on around him.

While the whole country was worrying about our image, Vogts seemed only concerned with results. Watching him on the huge screen of a multiplex cinema with the smell of popcorn wafting through the room was like watching an old movie from the Fifties in which sons call their fathers "sir". And it was only the beginning.

Act Three

On June 29th, Germany beat Mexico in the second round with two late goals saving a game that at one point had seemed beyond hope. Vogts and his players were talking of "morale" and "proverbial German virtues". Hundreds of journalists and roughly 25 million German TV viewers were talking of "luck" and "bloodless football". The former Kaiserslautern coach Karl-Heinz Feldkamp drily said: "We must not forget we could have met the Dutch in this game. And I don't want to think about what they would have done to our team."

By now, Vogts had already ousted sweeper Olaf Thon because, as he bizarrely explained, "Thon couldn't deal with the pressure of Matthäus's presence on the bench". And, more importantly, he had dropped Andreas Möller, who was seen as the main culprit for Germany's lack of creativity. Möller was brought on for the last 30 minutes of the Mexico game and again failed to make an impression. On the pitch, that is. Off the field he was suddenly the main story.

An irritated press and a dissatisfied public had seen the Dutch, the French and the Brazilians – even the English! – play modern, entertaining football and had found their own team dour and colourless.

But it was hard to argue with the fact that Germany were still in the competition, and so all that pent-up aggression suddenly came pouring down upon a hapless Möller, producing the ugliest three days of sports journalism I can recall. "Failure" was the nicest word used about him, "weakling" and "wimp" more common.

A television journalist demanded that Möller should never play for Germany again, and even the otherwise refreshingly objective Günter Netzer said he "would never come through as a world-class player". Then the newspaper *Bild* learned that Möller's wife had rung her husband, begging him to take the next flight home – and you can imagine what sort of leering, sarcastic headline that made. Vogts, asked about the situation, made things even worse by sneering: "Oh, you mean this 'Darling, come back to me' stuff?"

What saved Möller from having to declare his unconditional resignation and flee France in a horse-drawn carriage to seek refuge in the Tibetan mountains was the long-awaited catharsis – the quarterfinal against Croatia.

Act Four

They played a decent game for most of the first half. In fact they later claimed it had been their best performance so far, but that's not saying much. Then Wörns was sent off – and I have yet to meet anybody who does not agree the red card was justified. Then Croatia scored. Then Germany made asses of themselves by replacing Häßler and Hamann with Kirsten and Marschall so that they ended the match with six defenders and four target men. Then it was all over. And then the World Cup began all over again.

Because what happened in the half-hour following the final whistle put everything that had gone before – the media criticism, the hooligan problem and the Möller row – into the shade. The country knew very well that it was watching a fine World Cup and that the only spoilsports were the Germans. Every country had great fans except Germany (and England of course), which had thugs; most countries had played attacking, technically good football, except Germany, which had managed to fulfil every cliche you can come up with. "It's a good thing we lost," wrote a prominent paper the next day. "We had no business being there, alongside Holland and Brazil and France!"

That, indeed, was how the majority of people felt. And now they hoped for nothing more than a graceful exit so that the main actors could claim centre stage again. None of the players (not even Klinsmann) felt it was his duty to thank the fans who had sat through the ordeal. None felt they should officially congratulate their opponents for winning. Instead they stared into the cameras with contorted faces and accused the referee of robbing them. They moaned about "provocative play" by the Croatians. Wörns called his sending-off "a joke" and Suker "an actor". Jürgen Kohler even hissed that "such decisions always go against the Germans". But the icing on the cake was delivered by Vogts, who hinted there may have been "orders from above" to stop the Germans because "they have been too successful in the past".

Back home, millions of football fans stared at their TV sets in utter disbelief, many thinking, surely, what a great tournament this could have been without Germany. Over the next few days, the details of the game were almost forgotten. What dominated headlines, news reports and conversations was the behaviour of the squad. The mass-circulation tabloid *Bild* (still the most reliable indicator of the national mood) spat: **Stop Whining!** The sub-heading read: "Bad football. Bad losers." At the other end of the spectrum, the usually reserved and often near-comatose *Kicker* labelled the team's manner "unsportsmanlike, petty and paltry".

Another sports paper fell back upon sarcasm bordering on bad taste: "Vogts has created a new myth of the 'stab in the back' by claiming his troops are still unbeaten on the field of honour, but were betrayed by a Norwegian referee." This is a reference to the claim by proto-fascists of the 1920s that Germany lost the First World War only because the democratic politicians left in charge after the Kaiser's abdication in 1918 signed the terms of surrender, while the army was "undefeated in the field" – and yes, it is the most scathing thing ever written about a German national coach.

Seemingly the only inhabitant of this country still willing to think along Vogts's lines was Chancellor Kohl. "I think the referee lost the game," he said. "Why do they always punish us Germans?" Immediately, the magazine *Stern* jumped at the chance to turn his words back on himself: "This German team exactly mirrored the way Kohl runs the country: worn-out, stolid, uninspired and helpless," adding that "the true German virtues as revealed by this World Cup are: a tendency to whine, smugness and ignorance."

The epilogue was predictably anti-climactic. There were some meetings, some official statements, and still more meetings. There was the promise to bring young blood into the team and a thinly-veiled threat by some Bundesliga people to break away from the DFB if Vogts didn't stop blaming the league for his shortcomings. Vogts himself came around a few days later and said that he had got carried away, that he had apologised to FIFA and that, contrary to what everybody said at the time, he had visited the Croats' dressing room after the game to congratulate them. He also said: "The German is disappointed. The German didn't get into the semi-final." (I'm not making this up.) All of which, sadly enough, only proved that he still had no idea what was going on.

To the German multiplex-audience following the entertainment machine that was the World Cup, it didn't matter at all what Vogts had done or said in the privacy of a dressing room; it didn't even matter whether "a German" went out in the quarter-finals or the semis. To them, what mattered was what they saw on the screen.

And the image appearing there was not that of a graceful Beckenbauer putting his arms around Bobby Robson before the two men's teams began a penalty shoot-out. It wasn't even some bozo kissing another guy's bald head. It was just the face of the Ugly German. And in the background three fat tenors sang the worst-ever version of *You'll Never Walk Alone*. It ruined the whole film.

the lost boys

John Perlman

Saturday June 13th

"It's just a game," says the black woman to her workmate as she pushes the plastic bottles of full cream closer together, making space for the case of low-fat on the floor at her feet. "One must win and one must lose."

They are packing the refrigerated shelves at a suburban supermarket in Johannesburg, ahead of the weekend rush, but their minds are on the only thing that matters this morning. "Yes, one must win and one must lose," says the second woman with an angry toss of her braids. "But not like that. Where does he come from, that coach who made us play like that? France. And the player who scored two own goals? From France. And which team were we supposed to beat? France. One must win and one must lose, but not like that."

It's the morning after a 3-0 whipping by France in South Africa's first-ever World Cup finals game, and everywhere you go there are murmurings of gloom and mutterings of treachery. What was

Philippe Troussier, South Africa's charmless French coach, trying to achieve with such a defensive approach? And how could Pierre Issa, born in the former mining town of Germiston, east of Johannesburg, but raised in France, stick the ball in his own net not once but twice? Eventually lame jokes will raise a smile, like: "Knock knock. Who's there? Issa. Issa who? Issa goal." But not today.

Of course, nobody knows now that South Africa have just lost to the team that will win the World Cup, by the same score that will sink the mighty Brazil. But then in South Africa nobody shows much interest in any other team in the world except the all-dancing, all-dribbling, all-conquering (but oh-so-seldom straight-shooting) *Bafana Bafana*. "The Boys". Our boys.

South African journalists sent to France don't exactly help to broaden the perspective. The country's biggest newspaper group, Independent Newspapers, for instance, has four writers at the World Cup, but not one goes to the French camp to check out the opposition ahead of the match in Marseille. They don't bother visiting the Danes or the Saudis either.

Instead they faithfully relay and amplify all the pre-match promises of the country's heroes. "I believe we have a realistic chance of reaching the quarter-finals and after that don't write us off going all the way," says striker Benni McCarthy, who was tipped by former coach Jomo Sono to challenge for the Golden Boot alongside Ronaldo, Batistuta and Del Piero. "We could cause a huge upset and reach the final," says midfielder Helman Mkhalele. "My belief is that France are in for a big wake-up call," says Issa.

Anything anyone says about the South African team is reshaped into cheerleading headlines. An "umm, er, perhaps" sort of comment from Iceland's coach Gudjor Thordasson – who drew with *Bafana Bafana* 1-1 in a dismal pre-France friendly – appears as **Bafana Can Do It, Says Iceland Coach**. So too with Pelé's pre-tournament Mastercard press release, which includes the line: "I don't think South Africa, who played very well last year, will be easy to beat." This bit of non-committal politeness earns the headline

Pelé: Get Ready For Some Surprises And The Biggest Could Be Bafana Bafana.

Kick-off against France is at 9pm local time, but the city starts emptying and businesses wind down from mid-afternoon. A broadcast of the match on a massive screen at a drive-in perched on a mine dump above Johannesburg draws 15,000 people, who start packing the place long before the sun sets, and warm up by dancing to a string of top bands playing *kwaito* (the latest hard-edged township sounds).

With the players now incommunicado, and the always-cryptic Troussier growing odder by the day – "I have two options," he says, "attack or defend" – the ever-loyal hacks are having to scratch around for a last bit of good cheer. There is no Mandela magic this time around – the president is otherwise engaged, attending a meeting of the Organisation for African Unity before going on to the summit of the European Union. But the players, according the front page of Johannesburg daily the *Star*, have received "a huge boost" with the arrival in Marseille of deputy president Thabo Mbeki and sports minister Steve Tshwete. The French, no doubt, are really worried now.

It was always expected that South Africa would look to weather an early storm from *Les Bleus*. "The first 30 minutes could decide our World Cup," says Mark Fish. So the cagey, somewhat jittery play of *Bafana Bafana* gets some measure of sympathy at first. France lead 1-0 at half-time, but Issa comes close with a header just before the break. We're still in it.

But the second half is dismal – not just Issa's two own goals, but the complete absence of a team pattern and the glaring inadequacy of far too many players' technique. Well, I thought it was pretty obvious. One senior newspaper executive, having spent the day totting up the profits made on a nationwide "half-price *Bafana Bafana* special edition" rings the office after the final whistle and insists that the front-page headline should read **Buffoona Buffoona**. But shrewd editorial judgment prevails and they settle for **Oh No**

Bafana. After all, there are still two more games left and millions of papers to sell.

The afternoon after the night before sees Nigeria up against Spain. In a society where a sense of African brotherhood has given way to alarming and increasing levels of xenophobia as joblessness grows and government poverty programmes struggle to deliver, Nigerian immigrants are often enemy No 1, seen by many as con-artists and coke merchants. But today they are our brothers, as a thrilling 3-2 win shows just how wonderful and irresistible African football can be. *That* is the way we should be playing say the fans, the experts, the players in the squad. Like Africans. That the Nigerians are much better technically, more composed and intelligent, altogether better footballers, never comes up for discussion.

Back at the *Bafana Bafana* base camp in Vichy – speaking of treacherous Frenchmen – reserve striker Jerry Sikhosana says: "I appreciate what Philippe Troussier is doing for us, but at the end of the day we are not European players. We can't play like that. It's time to do our own thing and show the world what we are capable of."

Thursday June 18th

The *Bafana Bafana* players, according to one newspaper headline (**We'll Do It Our Way**), are planning to toss overboard the fancy ideas Troussier has tried to impose on them in his three months in charge, and play it South African-style against Denmark. No two people, of course, can quite agree on what that South African style actually is, although the verve of the Nigerians continues to be invoked as an example.

The omens as kick-off approaches aren't good. At Lord's, South Africa have lost four batsmen for less than 50 runs in the second Test against England, and the only thing falling faster than wickets is the currency, which begins what will be a steep and steady plunge against the dollar and the pound.

The Danes score early and come close to adding more before the break. When Mkhalele misses an open goal it looks like bye-bye

Bafana Bafana. But in the second half South Africa come back. McCarthy, at last, turns hype into reality, with a sweetly taken goal from close range. It's the first time – and sadly the last – that South Africa's midfielders and front men combine at pace, using trickery and skill for destruction, not decoration. A sweet, sweet goal. As the Danes flag in the heat, South Africa press forward. Two Danes are sent off, Alfred Phiri joins them for using an elbow, and then with virtually no time left, Quinton Fortune drives forward and shoots. The ball flies, swerves, dips, sets the crossbar shaking. It finishes 1-1.

We did it our way, all right, but what way was that? Fortune, for instance, outstanding against Denmark, learned some of his football growing up on the Flats outside Cape Town. But in his early teens he went to Spurs and then Chelsea, who sent him on to Atlético Madrid. An African player, yes, but a footballer immeasurably refined and improved by playing in Europe.

The day after the match, football has surrendered its grip on the front-page lead to the plunging rand, but the *Star* continues to find that little something that makes us such a special nation. The match report begins: "Benedict McCarthy took his first steps yesterday towards achieving international stardom."

Wednesday June 24th

On the Sunday before the decider against the Saudis, one of the newspapers broke the cosy conspiracy around the camp and reported that ten of the players had gone out and got plastered after the France match. A couple of days later, another daily reported that some of the squad had hired a couple of rooms which they used to screw around with the long queue of ever-willing Vichy groupies. And then it got worse. Striker Phil Masinga, initially ruled out of the Denmark match with an ankle injury, said Troussier forced him to play for the last few minutes of the match, despite the fact that he could hardly move. Sikhosana, enraged that the coach preferred "Hop-along" Masinga to "Legs of Thunder" Sikhosana, insisted that he be allowed to go home. And then it got worse.

Bafana Bid Hit By Split said the headline two days before the Saudi match. Striker Brendan Augustine and the aptly named midfielder Naughty Mokoena were sent home for breaking curfew again and disco-crawling until dawn. "In this squad there are only five players who don't need a father, a teacher or a policeman," said Troussier. "The team is not mature. I have received a message back from South Africa that they don't want a foreigner as coach. Perhaps it is time for me to go now."

Yes Boys, You Can says the front-page headline of the *Star* on matchday. **Sheikh And Destroy** counters the tabloid the *Sowetan*. But soon after Shaun Bartlett puts South Africa into the lead, Issa gives Saudi Arabia a penalty. Then Issa gives Saudi Arabia another penalty. The *Bafana Bafana* performance is spiritless, directionless, dispirited and lifts only briefly when Delron Buckley, a youngster based in the Bundesliga with VfL Bochum, comes on for his first World Cup appearance and tears repeatedly through the right side of the Saudi defence. What on earth has he been doing on the bench all tournament?

The silence over the Parc Lescure in Bordeaux is pretty much matched by the gloom in the Bass Line bar in Johannesburg. With the Saudis 2-1 up, and not much left of the 90 minutes, the punters have long since stopped imploring and beseeching, and all but given up grumbling. All that can be heard – via the tinny sound of two TVs the owners have managed to borrow from some regulars – is the sound of a man in the stands, singing a wailing Arabic dirge through a loudhailer. "Can't one of our fans go over and smack that singer," says a morose-looking man. "Apparently he's a top Saudi pop star," says his mate. "They call him al-Jarreau." Out of time, out of jokes, on our way out of the World Cup. In a funny way, it's almost come as a relief. From the ludicrous mix of arrogance and ignorance at the start, to the one-eyed insistence that all failures were the Frenchman's fault, we've been a divided, squabbling, short-sighted nation for most of the tournament. Not a pretty sight.

A late penalty gets South Africa a second World Cup point, but

Troussier's post-match words are blunt. "I was not only disappointed by the attitude of the team during the match, but also after the game. Instead of their heads being down after just being knocked out of the World Cup, everybody was fine. They were probably wondering where they were going to go out tonight."

Back home, the reflective mood is about more than just football. The dream of a new South Africa, a proud and successful Rainbow Nation, is not dead, but it is in need of resuscitation. *Bafana Bafana* in France were meant to provide it, the way they did in winning the 1996 African Cup of Nations. But that was a smaller stage, a home tournament, an easier task. And these are different times. Crime is rampant, employment is scarce and shrinking, and Mandela is in the last months of his fairytale presidency before handing over to Mbeki.

It is three years to the day since a South Africa united in exhilaration and some disbelief watched the Springboks win the rugby World Cup, watched Mandela dressed in a green and gold jersey hand the trophy over to the captain Francois Pienaar, both national icons wearing No 6. Mandela magic we all called it, a nation of miracle junkies always looking skywards for our next consignment of manna, as the ground at our feet grows more cluttered with tasks undone. As *Bafana Bafana* troop off the field, one punter in the Bass Line bar looks down into his beer and mutters: "Mbeki magic. We've got it."

The Aftermath

When the team arrive back, Troussier gets bundled into a police car and driven off, as a gang of fans rushes towards him, keen to discuss his failure to use the sweeper system. But it's not quite the mob some predicted. In a way, the players' gutless capitulation to the neat-but-nice Saudis took some of the heat off Troussier, focusing much-needed attention on some of the things that are wrong with South African players. The big question for the coming year is whether anyone will take the long, hard look at the domestic game that it so desperately needs. While the advertising/promotional cliche would have it that we are the Brazil of Africa, the truth is we are actually a nation alarmingly deficient in basic footballing technique.

With another Premier Soccer League season under way, the evidence is there at every match. Count the crosses from the flank that really penetrate. Add up the number of shots on target. There are some days when you won't need more than one hand. And what passes for skill is often merely decoration. Despite a month of watching World Cup football, players are still beating their man, then going back to beat him again if the first move gets a loud enough chorus of whistles.

There is still no development plan for South African football. And delight at news of a massive sponsorship from a mobile phone company is tempered – for me at least – by the details. A huge slice is to be spent on an annual fixture against a leading European team (Ajax are first up) in which the South African team will consist of one player from each of the top division clubs, selected by a fan phone-in. Much-needed millions destined to be spent, again, on meaningless marketing hype. Meanwhile, all over the country, dilapidated stadiums wait for someone to give grassroots football a home.

The World Cup debacle has exposed and reinforced deep divisions within South African football. Sentiment against foreign influences is strong, fuelled by columnists who write things like this: "The aliens have descended on our beloved game and they are wreaking havoc." Those lines of division will deepen when the new national coach is announced. There were only two South African applicants for the post in the initial round-up of candidates – Troussier's assistant Trott Moloto and national Under-23 coach Shakes Mashaba.

It is no secret that the leadership of the South African Football Association believes we need more international expertise. That view carried some weight when the list of names bandied about included Bora Milutinovic, Carlos Alberto Parreira and Ruud Gullit. But it was less convincing when the names in contention encompassed the Yugoslavs Miloslav Bjelica (no, I've no idea either) and Dusan Kondic (coached in the Angolan First Division), Eoin Hand (managed the Republic of Ireland), Ron Atkinson and Howard Wilkinson. It's that bad.

One thing did lift my spirits a little, though. At a lunchtime party held by some of my neighbours, a small black boy was kicking his ball around the garden. "Do you want to be like Doctor Khumalo?" asked one of the guests. "No, I want to be like Ronaldo," he said, and went back to his ball. At least some people here know where to set their sights.

blond bombshell

Richard Augood

It was a hell of a party.

Before the match against England, no one was in any doubt that this was the most important game of the group phase. Small beer, of course, compared with the confrontations that would inevitably come Romania's way in the knockout phase. After all, this was a team featuring the likes of Gheorge Hagi, Adrian Ilie, Gheorge Popescu, Doriel Munteanu and Dan Petrescu. Well, yes. As it turned out the stars were ambushed before they could get past the second round. It seemed no one had told them that the Croatia match was anything to be concerned about. Maybe the people knew that the victory over England was as good as it was going to get. Maybe they shared coach Anghel Iordanescu's hotline to God.

It was a hell of a party, even if it got off to an inauspicious start. Romania's final warm-up match, against Moldova, had to be moved from Bucharest to Ploiesti, the cradle of the Romanian game, after the Bucharest crowd booed the team off the pitch at the end of their

3-2 victory over Paraguay. The crowd was so hostile that goalkeeper Bogdan Stelea bared his back and gave the middle finger sign to the supporters behind his goal, while Dan Petrescu half-seriously suggested that Romania should play their home games in Bulgaria.

Time for the now-customary media blackout. In USA 94 the blackout had been declared after a Colombian TV crew was caught rummaging through the players' rooms. Only the threat of expulsion from the tournament persuaded Iordanescu and Hagi to give a few terse press conferences. This time they were, to coin a phrase, up against the enemy within. The increasingly salacious Romanian press was blamed by the players for stirring up resentment towards them. Deprived of drug scandals or nightclub shenanigans they chose to highlight the great wealth (astronomical relative to nearly all Romanians) of the team and to portray them as nothing more than mercenaries. Hagi's response was: "We work hard, why shouldn't we have a nice home and a nice car?"

It fell on deaf ears, though, and by the time the team set off, the media picture was of a bunch of greedy good-for-nothings who would take the pennies off a dead man's eyes. But then they beat Colombia, so everything was all right again.

Away from the feud with the squad, enthusiasm for the tournament was breaking out in the most unlikely places. Issue 400 of *20th Century*, the weighty cultural magazine funded by the Ministry of Culture, the Union of Romanian Writers and the Soros Foundation, was devoted entirely to football, featuring articles and excerpts by, among many others, Ludwig Wittgenstein, Mario Vargas Llosa, Nick Hornby and the French ambassador to Romania. And Desmond Morris, natch.

The Ministry of Culture also collaborated with the Bucharest branch of the British Council (as featured in the TV series *Fortunes of War*) to stage an exhibition in the National Gallery of Julian Germain's football photography, entitled *The Wonderful World of Football*. Good news indeed for the unnamed Blyth Spartan, whose penis has now been examined and commented upon by the great and good of Romanian society. And by a knot of giggling schoolgirls on the occasion I was there.

All through the build-up to the England game there had been a lot of discussion about "perfidious Albion" and its grumbling about Romania being the seeded team in the group; about its dismissal of the Romanian team as "past it"; and about its hooligans. "Greetings from beautiful Toulouse," wrote one correspondent, "which is full of tattoos and beerguts." Then it was reported that the day before the game ITN had run yet another story about Romanian orphanages. Perhaps justifiably there were complaints that the floods in rural areas which had claimed over 40 lives in the previous week were more of a legitimate news story, but that the British media would rather encourage contempt than sympathy for Romanians.

It was a hell of a party, which was just as well because the television coverage was desperate. Thanks to a law decreeing state television should have the rights to major sporting occasions, the coverage of all the matches was on TVR1 rather than the infinitely more slick ProTV, despite their offer of $1 million for the rights to show some of the games. TVR1 claimed that their stand was taken for egalitarian reasons. Cable station ProTV is only available to about 70 per cent of Romanian viewers. The games should be available to everyone, they said. Everyone knew that TVR1 was just taking a rare chance to flick the Vs at their competitors, having been out-performed on every level by the flash, American-backed upstarts ever since their launch a couple of years ago.

TVR1's opening titles consisted of a list of the FIFA-endorsed "finer points of the game", illustrated by flash-cuts of players representing each. Thus, for *suturi* (shots) we got Alan Shearer, for *driblinguri* (dribbles) we got Dennis Bergkamp and *fente* (fancy skills) was accompanied by footage of the old Hagi magic. Slightly more surprising was the choice of Demetrio Albertini to exemplify *actiune* (actions), and absolutely baffling was that to personify "fair play" (seemingly there is no Romanian phrase for this) they chose Andreas Möller.

Then, for the duration of the game, it was off with the sound and on with the (relative) sagacity of Graham Taylor on the BBC World Service. Romanian TV's big problem was that due to difficulties in obtaining accreditations the commentators were "doing a Eurosport" and commentating on the TV pictures ("You join us here in Malmö" – no we don't Archie, you're in a cupboard on Wardour Street). That said, there was no excuse for the discussion programmes.

After the success of their 6.06-style phone-in show during the domestic season, ProTV launched their World Cup special – three hours long, but without the rights to show so much as one second of footage from the games. Still, at least they could afford to draft in some heavyweight analysts, including ex-players and referees. Every one of the many other stations also adopted this format, but with neither footage nor informed analysis.

By all accounts there were more people out in Bucharest's Revolution Square to celebrate the victory over England than there had been during the 1989 revolution itself. Of course, there were no *Securitate* snipers firing into the crowd this time, which may have had something to do with it. Carling had wisely taken down their big banners exhorting people to drink the official lager of the FA Carling Premiership – a strange ad campaign here anyway, considering the only place you can buy the stuff is in the overpriced bars of business-traveller hotels.

The most conservative estimate is that there were about 200,000 people out, ten per cent of Bucharest's population. "Oli, ole, we beat the monkeys," many of them chanted, "Oli, ola, we beat England too." It rhymes in Romanian, as do the less brazenly racist "Don't forget this, England, your time has come too" and "Tell us, England, who is the leader?". Prime Minister Radu Vasile, on a state tour of Poland, had thrown a party for the journalists accompanying him and was only too happy to give interviews to them all after the match, looking forward to a dramatic increase in the feelgood factor.

The press went into overdrive, cataloguing all the perceived slights of the previous few days, crowing over the fact that it was the two England-based players, Petrescu and Viorel Moldovan, who had inflicted the damage and avenged the defeat in the 1970 World Cup. Many people were still out on the streets as others were on their way to work.

With England dispatched, the way was clear to a meeting with a beatable Croatia, then an easy dismissal of the geriatric Germans and their farcical goalkeeper, after which... And then, when the team came out to face Tunisia with their hair bleached, and soon-to-be-ex-General Iordanescu shaven-headed, everyone was certain. They had finally found the confidence, a lack of which had been the cause of their downfall against Ireland and Sweden in 1990 and 1994. So they only got a draw against Tunisia? As the pundits pointed out, that was all that was needed. What was the point of rushing around picking up bookings or injuries? Leave it to Iordanescu. He knows what he's doing.

It was a hell of a hangover. The performance against Croatia immediately set matters back to their pre-World Cup levels. The bunch of money-hungry bums who sleepwalked their way to capitulation had been haggling with the Romanian FA, demanding more money. **You Wanted More Money?** screamed the full-page headline of *Pro Sport* two days after the game, "You haven't been paid yet? It's because you played like idiots!" The only person to escape censure was the usual scapegoat, Bogdan Stelea, who perversely enough gave a barnstorming performance in the Romanian team's worst display of the past six years.

Significantly, he was the only one not to have participated in the hair nonsense, which we were told was the result of a bet between Iordanescu and the squad. What a stupid idea that was. Iordanescu had forgotten that Romanian teams thrive on perceiving themselves to be up against it. All their greatest results come when no one gives them a chance. Suddenly they start getting cocky and mess it all up.

When the team returned it got much, much worse. For some reason the entire population of Romania seemed not to know what

45

the rest of the world knew, namely that Romania's last game in France 98 was to be the last international appearance for Gica Hagi. As the team and Iordanescu made an appearance at the national stadium, a tearful Hagi stepped up to the microphone to announce to all present his retirement from the national team. The howls of anguish from the thousands present meant it took about four minutes for him to deliver his very short valedictory speech. An extremely long time even for someone as famously taciturn as "The Macedonian".

Apparently there was still a tournament going on in France, although you wouldn't have thought so, as the national angst gland went hyperactive. Television stations dedicated their schedules to Hagi retrospectives, a repeat of 1996's Gica Hagi tribute concert and interviews with the great man himself. The most revealing insight, apart from the fact that he comes across as a really nice guy, was that he had to ask his mum's permission to bleach his hair. "I don't really believe in that kind of thing. I don't even let my wife dye her hair," he said. "You know I don't approve of that kind of thing," he quoted his mum as saying, "but if you've promised all your friends, then I suppose you'll have to do it." He was completely shaven-headed by the time he returned to Romania.

Then Viorel Moldovan spoke to the press. Never one to keep his opinions to himself, he used the opportunity to wade into Iordanescu. After a few criticisms of the ex-coach's motivational, tactical and preparational methods he dropped his bombshell, exploding the myth about the bet. Moldovan revealed that the devoutly religious Iordanescu had phoned Father Argatu, a senior figure in the Romanian Orthodox Church, after the England match. Argatu apparently told Iordanescu that the game was up. God was no longer on their side. Astonishingly, Iordanescu then chose to communicate this information to the team. The bleaching and shaving of hair had been an attempt to break the jinx.

Immediately the press launched into a full-scale denunciation of Iordanescu's ludicrous superstition, his tactics, his preparation, his team selection and his decision to tell the team of Father Argatu's assertion. Then they remembered that, preoccupied with the woes of Hagi's retirement, they had overlooked the fact that Iordanescu had also quit to go and look after the Greek national team.

He was replaced by Victor Piturca, a man with minimal managerial experience, and who was banned from playing for a year in the early Eighties after a betting scandal. Not match-fixing, that was the job of the Ceausescus. Apparently he was caught playing poker for more money then most Romanians could hope to earn in ten years. A man against whom they'd waged a concerted and vitriolic campaign, seeking instead the appointment of his former Steaua team-mate Ladislau (Laszlo) Boloni.

Despite his savaging after the fiasco in France, it was Iordanescu who salvaged Romania's doomed campaign to qualify for USA 94. It was Iordanescu who led them to three consecutive tournaments. It was Iordanescu who won international respect for Romanian football. And now he and Hagi are gone. All concerned with Romanian football are terrified that they may have reached the end of their "Golden Epoch" and that it may be followed by a footballing decline of Hungarian proportions

It's a hell of a hangover. And it's probably going to be a long time before it passes.

winless wonders

David Roberts

Despite failing to win

a game in the tournament, the Chilean team returned from France 98 as heroes in the eyes of both the public and, almost without exception, the media. Thousands of people turned up at the airport on a bleak winter morning at the crack of dawn to welcome their idols, as the team – according to leading sports commentator Julio Martinez – united the country like never before.

Following a first round exit the last time Chile made it to the finals in 1982, acrimonious squabbles broke out between the media and the team, not least between Martinez himself and manager Luis Santibañez. But this time it was different. "The public forgave the team's errors," said Chile's equivalent to Jimmy Hill, referring to the 4-1 drubbing at the hands of Brazil in the second round. "And this is something we have never seen previously."

Once it became clear that Brazil would be Chile's second round opponents, the public all but resigned themselves to a noble defeat.

After all, somebody had to play Brazil, and given Chileans' sympathies towards the Brazilians in general – witness the 1994 World Cup final when there were celebrations on the streets of Santiago, in sharp contrast to Buenos Aires – that was as good a way as any to get knocked out. Indeed, after 16 years out of the World Cup, the mere act of qualifying for France was a major achievement. And reaching the second round was as far as any reasonably-minded person could expect.

But controversial former player and television critic Eduardo Bonvallet, who has been threatened with legal action more times than most commentators here have screeched "gooool", is not a reasonably-minded person. The sole dissident voice in a sea of eulogies, Bonvallet accused the team of being duped by the Brazilians. "They fell into a trap," he maintained, by taking the game to Brazil in the opening minutes, allowing themselves to be lulled into a false sense of security. Chile were then ill-prepared for the ensuing bombardment, which saw Brazil 3-0 up by half-time and the Chileans booking their seats back to Santiago.

Their mediocre performance in the final against France showed the mighty *Cariocas* – as they call them here, although the name strictly refers only to residents of Rio de Janeiro – were far from invincible. Despite his obvious self conviction (read: big head), Bonvallet's words of wisdom didn't seem so compelling when his little magnets representing players kept falling off his blackboard and he periodically broke off from his critique in the middle of a sentence to proclaim the virtues of cheap Chilean plonk.

Bonvallet was not the only offender, although in contrast to his outspokenness most of the TV coverage suffered from an excess of banality. It centred around endless interviews with fans in France, mainly consisting of questions like "Who's going to win the big match?" and answers like "Chile, of course, 3-0, 2-1, 4-2" or whatever. Accompanying programmes, even one called *Nothing to do with the World Cup*, gave saturation coverage to the tournament, but said next to nothing of interest to anyone with the intelligence of a condor. Leading politician Enrique Krauss, president of the Christian Democrat party, joined in the criticism of television shows, describing them colourfully as "coprolaliac" (talking shit, from the Greek *kópros* meaning dung and *lalia*, talk). A debate in Congress ensued.

To win the World Cup, one has to start modestly and build up to a crescendo, as France amply demonstrated. In the case of Chile, they started well and looked progressively shaky. Their first match, against Italy, was undoubtedly the team's finest hour. **Brilliant Debut, Italy Equalise With Highly Dubious Penalty** cried the popular *La Tercera*. "We were on the point of converting an old dream into reality – winning a match in the World Cup finals... something not achieved since 1962," noted *La Época*. Apart from that 1962 tournament, when they reached the semi-finals as hosts, Chile's only finals victories were a meaningless 5-2 win over the USA in 1950 and two group successes in 1930.

The press insisted after the Italy game that referee Bouchardeau of Niger, whose mystifying penalty award in the last minute got the Italians off the hook, had been expelled from the competition, destined never to take charge of a first class match again, banished by João Havelange, Sepp Blatter and the Queen of Sheba. Nevertheless, he turned up again a few days later as fourth official during the Jamaica-Argentina match, after receiving the support of Blatter.

Next came Austria, in a game both the press and the public regarded as being Chile's best chance of pocketing a win. Once again, however, the party was ruined by a late equaliser, just 40 seconds from the end of a poor match. **Damned To Agony**, screamed *La Tercera*. Inevitably, the referee again came under fire. Egypt's Gamal Ghandour failed to award Chile an obvious penalty after 52 minutes, insisted the paper, when Austria's Markus Schopp cleared with his arm from within the box.

President Eduardo Frei, pictured watching the game with his wife Martita and leading ministers, held his head in despair. Attempting to win political mileage? Maybe, but football is not a political issue in Chile. Left, right and centre; upper, middle or lower class – all are equally fanatical.

One refereeing decision that did not receive more than a passing mention in most of the press was the disallowing of Cameroon's second "goal" just minutes before the end of the 1-1 draw in their final group game. Referee Laszlo Vagner thankfully, from Chile's point of view, saw something nobody else did – an infringement on the part of an unnamed Cameroon player which meant Chile qualified for the second round at the expense of the Africans. When the much-appreciated Hungarian ref blew the final whistle, a fiesta erupted on the streets of Santiago and every other town and village along the 3,000 miles of Chile. The result, 270 arrests, dozens of police officers injured and one death.

The myth that Chile were a team doomed to ignominy had already been smashed, said sports magazine *El Gráfico*. Naturally there were others who saw the climax of the Cameroon game in a different light. Issa Hayatou, president of the Confederation of African Football, described François Omam Biyick's effort as "a perfectly valid goal". The African Players' Association even took the matter to court in an attempt to get Cameroon reinstated. Needless to say, the case was thrown out. Intoxicated by reaching the knockout stage, few Chileans had much sympathy to spare for the Cameroonians. "I don't care one grain of cumin if Mboma's header which put Omam Biyick through was clean... certainly there was no foul," said Aldo Schiappacasse in *El Gráfico*. "Poor Vagner will, no doubt, burn in hell... but I don't care."

Bonvallet, who predicted that Chile should easily beat Cameroon "because the Africans' feet will be sore after playing two matches in boots when they're not used to wearing shoes", resorted to more deplorable racist remarks after the game, which have made him the subject of a National Television Council inquiry. "More than four blacks shouldn't be allowed to play in one team because they start eating each other," he asserted.

It's difficult to assess how outraged the average viewer was. Everyone knows Bonvallet sets out to shock – that is the main reason his programme is so popular – and racism is not a major issue in this relatively homogeneous nation. It is quite common among friends and family to refer to someone with a slightly dark skin as "blackie", or a person with a hint of oriental features as a "Chinaman". Witness tennis ace Marcelo Ríos, known affectionately as "Chino". (Although when a reporter once asked him if he had Indian blood in him, Rios replied: "And you're a son-of-a-bitch, too".)

As for the players themselves, team captain Iván Zamorano, the gentleman that he is, did nothing to jeopardise his status as the real darling of the media, despite Marcelo Salas's four goals. At 31, Zamorano almost certainly saw his last chance of getting a World Cup goal go up in smoke when he blasted a late free-kick against Brazil just wide. The manager, Nelson "Baldy" Acosta, is also now a national hero, even though the head of the Chilean Football Association, Ricardo Abumohor, said he would only serve until the end of the year. If it went to a general election, the public would undoubtedly give Acosta their vote of confidence. The naturalised Uruguayan took charge after the team could only draw against Venezuela in their first qualifying match for France 98 and led Chile to heights unseen in 36 years.

"We've turned the tide of history," said Acosta as the celebrations extended through the night after the draw with Cameroon. Thousands even came out on to the streets to honk horns, wave flags and blow trumpets after getting thrashed by Brazil. Their goals may have been modest, but for Chile, as Salas put it, France 98 was "mission accomplished".

heroics take a holiday

Gary Oliver

On Tuesday June 23rd,

most Scots arose with a spring in their step – England had just lost to Romania. Such English discomfort always gladdens many a Scottish heart. This time, though, there was also the small matter of a momentous evening ahead: for the first time in eight attempts, Scotland were to progress to the second round of the World Cup.

Unlike previous occasions, the Scottish team went into the final group match not having control over its own destiny. Nevertheless, journalists and pundits were unanimous in sensing the hand of history on their shoulders. Little did they realise it was merely poised to go for the jugular. The nagging fear was that Brazil, with the leadership of Group A already under lock and key, might turn out against Norway in flip-flops. The press, however, promised that Brazilian coach Mario Zagallo was eager to silence his Norwegian counterpart, the bumptious Egil Olsen having asserted that he could transform Brazil into a much more effective unit.

Scotland's players obviously swallowed this assurance. "If Norway beat Brazil there should be a stewards' enquiry," Craig Burley maintained. Nor was the threat posed by Morocco taken too seriously, even though Hadji and his mates had already caused a few blushes in Norway's defence. Dispatches from the front instead reported unrest in the Moroccan camp, the squad's spirit reputedly broken by their 3-0 loss to Brazil. And with much-ridiculed Driss Benzekri expected to keep goal wearing a red nose, there was a widespread assumption that the north Africans would be swatted aside.

Craig Brown, at least, was a little more circumspect: "I hear there is a lot of euphoria back home," he said. "I think we need to calm things down a little until the objective has been achieved." Unfortunately, the manager's caution went largely unheeded, and Scottish football went through its most hubristic few days for two decades.

True, the misplaced confidence lacked the sustained bombast of 20 years earlier. And Scotland's domination of Norway did provide understandable cause for optimism. The fact was, however, that the Scots failed to capitalise on overwhelming superiority – indeed, they had recorded no victory whatsoever since the final qualifying tie. Scotland's final outing on home soil was a feeble 1-1 draw against Finland yet, despite the novelty of the capital staging a full international, the team still struggled to fill Easter Road to its capacity of only 16,000. To a clearly apathetic public, the imminent World Cup campaign had become an exercise in damage limitation.

Goalkeeper Andy Goram was soon preoccupied with some damage limitation of his own. No sooner had the squad set up camp in America than Andy, not for the first time, declared himself mentally unattuned to play, a state of mind caused by the tabloids back home once more catching up with his extra-curricular activities. While SFA chief executive Jim Farry dismissed Goram as "yesterday's man", Brown remained remarkably sanguine, regarding his goalkeeper's withdrawal as "quite honourable".

Perhaps Brown felt some relief at having his most difficult selection decision – ageing Jim Leighton or declining Andy Goram? – made for him.

As Goram retired to a modest guest house on Blackpool's Golden Mile – he watched the tournament in a nearby boozer – his erstwhile colleagues prepared Stateside with two games. The matches yielded no wins, naturally, but draws with USA and Colombia, 0-0 and 2-2 respectively, did suddenly brighten up the mood. The opponents' insipid performances in France subsequently put those results into perspective. At the time, however, from the other side of the Atlantic, distance lent enchantment. The squad, press and public all began to exude more confidence than they had any right to, considering that Brazil lay in wait.

Brown took credit for the predictable plucky defeat against the world champions, but promptly blew most of it with his subsequent caution in the game against Norway. Above all, the Scottish media agonised over the choice of position for Craig Burley. The Celtic man longed to reprise his midfield club role and spent most of the tournament muttering "I'm not a full-back and I'm not a wing-back" to any journalist sympathetic to his argument. Which was most of them.

Not until Scotland were chasing the game against Norway did the manager finally instruct the dentally-challenged Burley to augment an attack which looked equally toothless. "I'm hoping [my goal] proved a little point to a few people," he mused. Brown attempted to deflect this, and other, criticisms of his formation by insisting: "We couldn't have started with the system we ended up playing." Why a line-up which dominated the close of a match would not also have controlled the opening was not entirely clear. The welcome suspension of Darren Jackson for the final group match gave Brown little option but to accede to the wishes of Burley and his media claque. Burley did, of course, proceed to make history against Morocco, but for entirely the wrong reason, entering the annals as the first bottle-blond ever to be sent off for Scotland.

Burley's folly put the tin lid on what was a deplorable team performance. Time and again Jim Leighton and his defenders were left horribly exposed. Leighton – a giant throughout the qualifiers – suddenly looked every one of his 40 years. In truth, the Scots were lucky to escape with only a three-goal beating, and Brown conceded, with masterly understatement, that Morocco had been the better side. As ever, though, he had at his disposal some fatuous match statistic: Scotland, apparently, gained five corners to Morocco's one.

Carrying out an immediate post-mortem, BBC Scotland's analyst Willie Miller harked back to the pivotal match against Norway. Scotland, he declared, had lacked "the right man, in the right place, at the right time". His comments were made all the more resonant by the presence at his shoulder of one Alistair McCoist. Even those of us allergic to Ally and his self-satisfied persona found it difficult to understand the housewives' favourite being confined to a TV studio.

Worse, Ally's exclusion from the squad also raised the unnerving prospect of his phizog being constantly on screen throughout the tournament. Always a man with a healthy conceit of himself, McCoist's nationwide broadcasts this time registered slightly lower than usual on the smug-o-meter. Hell, I almost warmed to the man when, during USA v Iran, he described a penalty box melee as a "stramash", probably the first non-ironic use of the auld Scots noun for about 15 years, since *Scotsport*'s much-loved Arthur Montford hung up his microphone.

Even so, the rest of the UK ought to be thankful it receives just small doses of this unfailing cockiness: such is his media profile in Scotland, McCoist makes Carol Vorderman seem like a recluse. His portfolio includes a low-rent chat show co-hosted with Fred MacAulay. The comedian – that's MacAuley by the way – is professional enough to just about hold things together. McCoist, on the other hand, proves conclusively that an impish grin is a flimsy foundation upon which to build a career in light entertainment.

That did not prevent BBC Scotland broadcasting from Paris a special eve-of-tournament edition, the pitiful quality of which one may judge from a guest list that included Ulrika Jonsson. (It was after the recording of this tomfool programme that her former beau Stan Collymore perpetrated his much publicised assault.) Also joining Ally and Fred from the C-list was Jimmy Hill, the traditional pantomime villain for a Scottish audience. Never mind that, apart from a 16-year-old reference to David Narey's "toe-poke" goal against Brazil, few of Hill's critics could quote him disparaging the Jocks.

Hill's unpardonable sin is to be perceived as an English cheer-leader. Displaying the cross of St George on that bow-tie simply reinforces his reputation as a latter-day Ken Bailey. Dotty he may now be, yet Jim is still not quite as confused as was the shambling Bobby Robson over on ITV. Watching a re-run of Chile's second goal against Italy, jaws slackened all over Scotland when Bob declared that Marcelo Salas's remarkable leap above Cannavaro reminded him of David Speedie (international appearances: ten; goals: 0).

Out-rambled by Robson, Hill also lost, temporarily, his mantle of Scotland's *bête noire*. For several days he was succeeded as devil incarnate by Tony Banks, the minister for sport committing the double whammy of being, (a) scornful of the self-styled Greatest Support in the World, and (b) an Englishman. A professional wiseguy, it is usually impossible to judge whether Tone is being earnest or taking the piss. However, in the context of the offending interview he gave to David Frost, his assertion that Scots behave impeccably merely to show up the English did sound a jocular throwaway line. Either that, or he is surreptitiously acting as recruiting sergeant for the SNP.

Yet even if Banks was not deadly serious, the comment contains a hint of truth. The Scottish press enjoys nothing more than to piously juxtapose the burlesque Scot with the snarling English thug. Thus, outraged tabloids made Banks's "gaffe" front-page news, the minister's future career prospects deemed the most pressing issue of the day. At such times, one wonders whether there exists on this planet a more thin-skinned and insecure nation, particularly where its football team and supporters are concerned.

That brouhaha made it even less likely that Scots would heed the touching advice of their compatriot John Gorman to root for England during the second phase. The general reaction to his plea was one of incredulity. Yet an NOP survey conducted in the wake of Scotland's exit found 60 per cent of Scots hoping England would succeed – an extraordinary, though improbable, conclusion. If the Anglophile contingent does indeed constitute the majority, it is, literally, a silent one. Brave is the man who would cheer an England goal while spectating in a Glasgow pub.

It is safe to assume our Bravehearts in France were not among those polled. On the eve of the crunch game against Morocco, and minutes after Romania's defeat of England, BBC Scotland unwisely broadcast from the centre of St-Etienne. Dougie Donnelly, Gordon Smith and Willie Miller were largely inaudible above a soundtrack of "Let's All Laugh At England" and "England's Coming Home". Which might seem reasonable enough. Note, however, that even 24 hours before Scotland's putative qualification, the Tartan Army's preoccupation was with England going home, rather than with rivals Norway or Morocco.

Nor were many in the media likely to be part of the 60 per cent humming *Land of Hope and Glory*. It would appear to have been enshrined in Scots law that during a World Cup or European Championship, every sports desk must keep a media watch, its purpose being to log gratuitous references to England and take umbrage at any perceived slight on Scotland. And it was perhaps symbolic that Tony Banks should be joined in the "news" pages by three pot-bellied pigs from Glasgow's Calderpark Zoo. The trio had been named Egil (Olsen), he having the temerity to call Scotland the poorest side in Group A; Martin (O'Neill), reputed to have wished for the Scots to be on the first plane home; and Jimmy, in honour of... go on, guess.

All of which was, no doubt, highly amusing for the zookeepers.

Yet this froth was reported as though it were a retort on behalf of an affronted nation. The orthodox line, which Tony Banks and other villains should have taken, was summed up by Goldenbollocks McCoist: "If there was a World Cup for fans, Scotland would beat Jamaica 4-3 in the final." This Ceilidh Boyz image is in some respects admirable. But the flip side is that the ethos of win-or-lose-let's-party places on the team no real demands or expectations. Thus, viewers back home suffered the grotesque spectacle of the players being cheered from the pitch in St-Etienne. Granted, events elsewhere ultimately rendered the defeat irrelevant. But Scotland had been pulverised long before there was any hint of a shock win for Norway at the Vélodrome.

With Group A producing, in Norway, by far the weakest qualifier, the feeling persists that Scotland had their best ever chance to progress, and muffed it. With ample opportunity to kill off the Scandinavians, Scotland proved neither sharp nor ruthless enough. Craig Brown would, no doubt, remind us that Norway came to the finals ranked seventh in the world. However, in football there are lies, damned lies and FIFA rankings.

Brown is not a manager to arouse adulation. But it is only fair to point out that his achievements – reaching both the European Championship and World Cup finals with the poorest crop of players in memory – have tended to be undervalued. He is, moreover, uniquely handicapped, managing a country in which the perennial champion club shows no inclination to develop native talent.

Brown remains unassailable. He will know, however, that most other coaches who failed to register a win in France returned home seeking alternative employment. Scotland, accustomed to such letdowns, likes to think it has a patent on heroic failure. Unfortunately, France 98 will be remembered not for heroism, just failure. And that from a line-up bullishly described by Brown before the tournament as being "every bit as good as England".

Curious, then, that Messrs Beckham, Ince and Batty should have brought more cheer to Scotland than anyone wearing dark blue. One French newspaper, overwhelmed by the euphoric reaction to the hosts' triumph, apparently described the outpouring of emotion as "a national orgasm". We Scots, meanwhile, looked on enviously, clutching our prescriptions for Viagra.

rebirth of a nation

Renato Pandža

For Croatia,

perhaps more than any other country at France 98, the World Cup was about more than football. Ever since its independence in 1991, sport has been one of the key elements in establishing the new state's identity and making the world aware of who the Croats are. Like so many of the states formed by the break-up of the Soviet Union and Yugoslavia, recognition by FIFA was second only in importance to a seat at the United Nations as one of the essential trappings of independence.

Since then, Croatia has eagerly pursued every possible avenue of sporting success, but in truth the cachet to be earned from providing the European club champions at water polo and handball is limited. Even basketball, where stars such as Toni Kukoc have made it big in the NBA, does not cut much ice in most of Europe -- and it is above all as a member of the European family of nations that Croatia aspires to be recognised.

So World Cup coach Miroslav "Ciro" Blazevic was quite serious when he said that one of the most important issues for the national team was to spread the word about Croatia around the world. Perhaps part of his motivation was to identify himself even more directly with President Franjo Tudjman (although it is hard to imagine how they could be closer than they already are), whose political future may also have been rescued by the team's success in France. Tudjman has seen football as a vehicle for his brand of nationalism ever since taking office, although not always with the desired results – his insistence that Dinamo Zagreb change their name to Croatia Zagreb is still bitterly resented by fans of the club.

During the World Cup, Tudjman and his highly unpopular government took every possible opportunity to be seen with the team and at the matches, so much so that some serious political analysts even claimed they were thinking of calling a snap election to cash in on the wave of national euphoria. Opposition politicians certainly took the threat seriously enough, visiting the players in France themselves in an attempt to blur the strong identification between Tudjman, the coach and the national side.

If many of the team's supporters were lukewarm about the political hangers-on in France, Blazevic himself inspired something approaching contempt before the tournament started. Few chants were heard more frequently in the qualifying and warm-up games than the old stand-by: "Ciro is a homosexual!" What began as a straightforward insult, however, gradually turned into something of a self-mocking dialogue as Blazevic's team marched through the rounds to the semi-finals. Graffiti appeared in Zagreb proclaiming: "We are the homosexuals – Ciro is our master!" or "We are the homosexuals, Ciro is ours!".

Such brazen displays of national sexual neuroses aside, Croatia's build-up to the tournament was little different to that of most other countries although, as a World Cup debutant, the coverage was somewhat more intensive. The squad's training sessions made the front pages, while the fans were preoccupied with procuring tickets from a recalcitrant FA. The owners of pubs and cafes bought new TVs for their terraces. Many firms did the same, knowing full well that all male and many female workers would otherwise follow Croatian tradition and phone in sick on match days. Two local breweries and one multinational drinks company started the biggest advertising campaigns ever seen in Croatia. Other companies followed, offering tickets for the World Cup matches as inducements for their consumers – which helped to explain why so few were left over for the supporters.

Naturally enough, the streets of Zagreb were deserted once Croatia's games started. The only exceptions were in two city-centre squares (Flowers Square and, appropriately enough, French Republic Square) where giant video screens had been erected. Both were packed with fans in national team shirts and painted faces. After the group wins against Jamaica and Japan all the major cities exploded, with people dancing and singing, climbing on monuments and jumping into the fountains.

Not so unusual in many cities, perhaps, but it was something of a new experience for Zagreb. Croatia's capital traditionally cultivates a cool and sophisticated image, leaning towards the mentality of Austria and central Europe in contrast to the (theoretically) warmer and more excitable Mediterranean parts of the country, specifically the Dalmation coast. A dozen years ago, street celebrations of any kind were almost unheard of in Zagreb. People there would have been ashamed to indulge in such crazy behaviour. Even the greatest successes of Zagreb sports teams were generally celebrated only around the stadiums or inside cafes. In Split, however, it was completely normal for university professors and other pillars of respectability to join the exuberant crowds on the streets when the football or basketball team won something.

That division changed partly because of the war. So many refugees arrived in the big cities from distant parts of the country that it is now almost impossible to talk, even in general terms, about the "typical" mentality of one part of the country or another. Now everything is mixed – urban with rural, north with south – and even Zagreb is learning how to enjoy itself.

More surprising changes were on the way in national attitudes that once seemed to be set in stone. Women, for example, took a greater interest in football than ever before. Even a few years ago the sight of a woman at a match in Croatia was as rare as snow in the Sahara. Yet during the World Cup they joined in as enthusiastically as any regular supporters – and were accepted as such.

Blazevic's egotistical posturing, which had done much to alienate the fans before the tournament, suddenly seemed to make sense after the success of the group games. "I want England and I know why!" he blustered. "They don't respect us!" With each victory the mood became more euphoric, the celebrations more intense. After the 1-0 win over Romania in the second round, police patrolled the streets warning people to stay indoors until the wild shooting from hundreds of guns had died down – a Croatian tradition that predates the war, incidentally.

But this was nothing compared to the unforgettable night after the victory against Germany. Many optimistic fans had hoped that Croatia might win, but none could have expected such a glorious triumph. **Croatia Is A Football Superpower** thundered the national daily *Jutarnji list* immodestly. **The Myth Of The German Untouchables Is Ruined** crowed *Slobodna Dalmacija*. In Zagreb alone more than 100,000 people squeezed into the main square to celebrate. Young and old, families and teenagers, men and women – no one wanted to miss this one. People were dancing on car roofs and jumping almost naked into the fountains. Dozens of cafes ran out of alcohol before the night was over.

A great drunken party, for sure, but one that may prove to be more significant than the majority of drunken parties that went on around the world during France 98. The performances of the team in France changed the normal atmosphere of the country. Even some quite serious sociologists argued that a mere football tournament was enough in itself to draw a line under the years of apathy that followed the war and the subsequent economic problems. Suddenly people were happy simply to talk football.

The most striking example was an ongoing protest by pensioners against government policy. Most of their final statement appealing to Tudjman for improvements to their lot was taken up with references to Croatia's success in the World Cup. Naturally, shops of every description also adopted a World Cup theme, decking themselves out in the red-and-white checks or France 98 symbols. Even the older women who serve behind the counter in Croatia's biggest chain store were not immune from the national mood, donning their football shirts like everyone else.

The image of the plucky little upstart nation taking on the world's football giants and giving them a beating was one eagerly fostered at home, and uncritically taken up in many other parts of the world. Yet for many Croats the success of their team in France also had a slightly darker undercurrent – the burning desire to outperform Yugoslavia. Although we heard that many people there were supporting Croatia after their own team was eliminated, few could find it in themselves to reciprocate such feelings. And when Holland eliminated Yugoslavia there was a further rash of celebratory shootings across Croatia.

The difference between the two is fairly simple to explain. Whatever the causes of the civil war in Yugoslavia, it is a fact that it took place almost exclusively on the territory of Bosnia, Croatia and (briefly) Slovenia. The vast majority of Serbs, whose government was cast as the aggressor by the international community, did not experience the troubles of the war directly, on their own land. That made it possible for them to forget the bad blood between the two countries and support Croatia. The Croats could not do so. In Bordeaux, before Croatia met Romania, we already knew that Holland had beaten Yugoslavia. One Croatian supporter said: "Even if we lose today, we are staying in France at least a day more than the Serbs."

As it turned out, Croatia stayed even longer than that, almost to the

bitter end. And even after the disappointment of the semi-final there was more to come with victory in the third-place match. Again, upwards of 80,000 people packed French Republic Square in Zagreb to welcome back the players. They were celebrating not just footballing success, of course, but something more. Something like the arrival of their country in the consciousness of the rest of the world. **President Tudjman Honours Heroes** wrote the Zagreb-based daily *Vecernji list*. And well he might have. Even in his wildest dreams he could not have counted on such an impressive contribution to his political future.

patriot games

Phil Ball

If it did nothing else

for Spain, the 1998 World Cup may at least have been responsible for hanging new pictures of national stereotypes in the galleries of our minds. Whatever happened to that nation of happy-go-lucky *mañana* merchants, scurrying around uselessly in John Cleese's kitchen, or to those moustachioed *matadores*, chatting in the heat of the afternoon sun? Spain, whose curiously pragmatic dullness during France 98 will squat heavily on the country's self-image for years to come, were at the very least true to Drake's famous dismissal: "There is plenty of time to win this game, and to thrash the Spaniards too."

Of course, nobody actually thrashed them, the opening game against Nigeria being the only one they (narrowly) lost. Indeed, their pyrrhic 6-1 destruction of Bulgaria, after the draw with Paraguay, represents the country's biggest win in its World Cup history. And yet the abiding image of the new Spain, in case you ever really believed in the old one, is of Atlético Madrid's Kiko, the Gascoigne among the lads, the whoopee-cushion joker of the pack, casually slotting home his side's sixth goal against the hapless Bulgarians, tears in his eyes as the news of Paraguay's third goal drizzled miserably down onto the Lens pitch.

This is not a sympathetic land. Jan Morris's observation that the Spanish are "destined to acts of cruelty against their own kind" was never better illustrated than in the football press's tactics throughout the campaign. The rat-pack, eager for revenge after Spain's good showing at Euro 96 had dented their campaign to oust manager Javier Clemente, began the French operation by opting for trench-warfare, firing a few shots across no-man's land in the vague hope of provoking the enemy into action. But as soon as the Nigeria game was over, the foot-soldiers went up and over, and the sniping turned into open warfare.

Marca's Julian Ruiz, long a Clemente-hater, went straight for the throat. "Clemente left out Amor. He didn't play with a recognised striker. He didn't use the wings. He went against his own philosophy. Excessive pride is a deadly sin, and it has no place in football." And all this despite the fact that Spain had really played quite reasonably, up to and even after Andoni Zubizarreta's fatal own goal. Other sections of the press were equally unforgiving, and the fact that this was the first time in 37 games that Spain had conceded three goals was completely forgotten in a dispropor-tionate torrent of criticism. Nevertheless, Ruiz's comically doom-laden words after that 2-3 defeat were to prove prophetic: "A green ghost hovers over our national spirit. Too many dreams – and dreams do not play football."

The green ghost of Nigeria was indeed to prove the psychological undoing of the side, for it played into the hands of Spanish fatalism – the idea that the world is somehow a lottery, and if the prizes don't come your way it is just a matter of bad luck. Spain trooped off the pitch in Nantes that sunny afternoon almost at five o'clock French time, echoing the lines of the poet Federico García Lorca that any Spaniard can quote:

A las cinco de la tarde
Eran las cinco en punto de la tarde
Un niño trajó la blanca sábana
A las cinco de la tarde

At five in the afternoon
It was dead on five in the afternoon
A boy brought out a white sheet
At five in the afternoon

The poem is a lament for the greatest of all Spanish bullfighters, Ignacio Sánchez Mejias, killed in the bullring 70 years ago. Such is the passion for football in Spain, and so heavy is its metaphoric touch to a people brought up on a diet of self-questioning, that the lines may soon re-enter the national consciousness as a requiem to the lost hopes of 1998, the year when the Spanish really thought they could win something.

The squad set off for France with the ill-advised words of Prime Minister José María Aznar ringing in their ears: "I hope the squad will reflect the up-and-coming power of the new Spanish nation," he proclaimed rashly. Two days after the Nigeria defeat, Aznar was on the hotline from Madrid to an unhappy Clemente, desperately trying to explain that the papers had quoted him out of context and that he hadn't meant to further dampen the players' spirits by saying that the squad had "paid the price for convincing itself that everything was going to be plain sailing".

But while the clumsy interventions of an inexperienced prime minister may have been unwelcome, Clemente's major irritants, as ever, were to be found in the media. To understand their hostility towards him, a little background is required.

Spain is a loose federation of quite distinct cultures, but there exist certain elements, as in many countries, who would prefer this not to be the case. The football tabloid *Marca* is, depressingly, the best-selling paper in Spain. In a country where the per capita purchase of newspapers and books is the lowest in Europe, *Marca* shifts some four million copies a day. The paper is based in Madrid, and its sentiments belong to a centralised vision of Spain, with Real Madrid as masters of the universe. Its timid critique of the hooligan *Ultra Sur's* antics during the 1998 Champions League semi-final in the Bernabeu raised old questions as to the real sentiments and affiliations of some of its journalists.

Marca has routinely questioned the fact that the Spanish senior national team and the Under-18s are both run by Basques, and returned to this bugbear just before the tournament began. At the end of an otherwise reasonable interview, the journalist asked whether Clemente thought it strange that he should be the national manager, given his affiliation with the centre-right Basque nationalist Partido Nacional Vasco. "Not at all," he replied, as affably as a reply can appear on paper. The journalist took another step: "And what of the fact that your sister is married to an alleged ETA activist?" This time less affably: "And what's that got to do with me? You want me to decide who my sister hangs out with?"

Clemente's successful record with the national side has stuck in the craw of the dominant Madrid press for years. On becoming national manager several years after a Clough-like injury prematurely ended his playing career, he soon earned a reputation for Clough-like dismissals of media fools. But unlike his closest English equivalent, he never became a media darling, or master of the TV-friendly quip. Dogged by his own stubborn nature, the feeling began to develop, even in those circles more favourably disposed to him, that his team selections were mere rebuttals of the line-ups proposed by *Marca's* journalists.

On the eve of the Paraguay match, he announced defiantly that the team would consist of "Zubizarreta plus ten others". His friend played well in that particular game, but most observers had been calling for the ageing goalkeeper's head from well before Euro 96. The ex-Real Madrid and Spain midfielder Michel said as much during his concluding remarks after the Bulgaria game on TVE1, the main Spanish channel. Michel, articulate and handsome in an Armani kind of way, had more reason than most to be unfavourable towards Clemente, for it was the latter who effectively ended his international career and those of the other members of the *quinta* (Sanchís, Buyo, Butragueño and Chendo being the others), a group of established Real Madrid players who represented an internal threat to Clemente's new regime. They have never forgiven Clemente, especially considering the large numbers of Basques (and Catalans) who were subsequently brought in to wear the national colours.

Michel, restrained by the medium of television, merely observed that it was a tragedy that Spain should have bowed out so early, and that the squad, overflowing with talent, had not been allowed to express itself. You do not have to subscribe to the Madrid conspiracy theories to agree with him. His co-summariser José Marí Bakero, who mumbled inaudibly into his chest for the duration of the tournament, muttered something about never recovering from the Nigeria game, but as teacher's pet to Clemente, and a Basque to boot, he was unlikely to rush in where Michel had feared to tread.

Immediately after the game, as the post-mortems began, the cameras cut back to Matias Prats, easily the pick of the TV journalists, standing with an old and crooked Alfredo Di Stefano, surrounded by the empty seats and ghostly light of the Félix Bollaert stadium in Lens. "It all went wrong from the beginning," the old man croaked, some fire still in his eyes. "Why begin a tournament with such a defensive line-up, when the best players are all forwards?" Why indeed?

The next morning *As*, *Marca*'s brother-in-arms tabloid, was predictably in full cry. **Javi, Piérdete!** screamed the headline (Javier, Go and Get Lost!) while *Marca* confined itself to **Día De Luto Nacional** (Day of National Mourning). *Sport*, a Catalan football tabloid, showed slightly more imagination on its cover, with a clever picture of several of the players crammed into a life-raft, the Titanic sinking behind them in the night with the word **Hundidos**

(Sunk) in large yellow letters above the scene. The designer of the page had managed to contrive the picture so that Zubizarreta appeared to be dropping Betis's Alfonso into the water – a cruel commentary on a goalkeeper who, whether you rate him or not, had just bowed gracefully off the scene with 126 caps to his name. Still, had his bosom pal Clemente finally dropped "little old bridge" (the meaning of his surname in Basque) after the Nigeria game, he would have retired one short of Shilton's then-record 125. More grist to the conspiracy theorists' mill.

Nevertheless, it would be too simplistic to attribute criticism of Clemente solely to the existence of Castillian-Basque tensions. The notion that a defeat of the Spanish national side is greeted with wild celebration on the streets of Catalunia and the Basque country is a myth perpetrated by those who have never lived here. Quite apart from the fact that the players from these two autonomous regions constituted 14 of the final squad of 22 (eight Catalans, six Basques), the average citizen from these regions has no one else to support, and neutrality is not a commonly used word in the Iberian lexicon.

In the radical leftist nationalist bars of the Basque country, of course, no one would wish to be seen supporting the enemy, and in both regions to walk around with the national side's nylon replica hugging the torso would be interpreted as an openly political statement. But even *El Correo*, published in Clemente's home city of Bilbao, began to question its most famous son. After the Bulgaria game, their editorial asked whether the fact that everyone accuses people from Bilbao of being big-heads could now be laid at the door of "our charming manager".

In a similar vein, *El Diario Vasco*, published in San Sebastián, led its sports section with **Se Consumó El Fracaso** (Failure is Complete), cruelly employing the word *fracaso* as a deliberate swipe at Clemente's famous and oft-repeated refrain that "failure is not a word in my vocabulary". The word was to crop up over and over again in the days following Spain's premature elimination, like some incessant chant at a wake.

Four hundred years after the sermon of Don Quijote – that the weakness of the Spanish is their inability to laugh at themselves – the lesson rings as true as ever. Self-parody requires self-analysis, and after several days of mud-slinging the media began to look for mitigating circumstances of the wrong sort. Instead of sticking to the more likely truths, that Clemente should have brought along the brilliant De La Peña, dropped Pizzi much earlier, played Morientes and Nadal from the beginning and so on and so forth, respectable papers such as *El País* and *El Mundo* began to clutch at straws, peddling a series of "facts" which they hoped might turn the tide of national pain more easily than could the simple acceptance of defeat. Peter Rufai, Nigeria's goalkeeper, was suddenly rumoured to have been bought off by the Paraguayans, despite the (unmentioned) fact that his personal fortune probably exceeded that of Paraguay's national debt. And Nigeria "didn't really try", did they?

In the *Guardian*'s summing-up of the tournament only one of their ten journalists picked a Spanish player, Hierro, for their personal World Cup XI. One out of 110 – a poor exam result. The mark could and should have been much higher. Interestingly, four of the writers rated Spain as their "biggest disappointment" and six of them chose Spain v Nigeria as the best game of the finals.

It will be of some compensation to the Spanish to know that international expectations of them had been high. Right from the beginning, this superstitious country was itself determined not to express too much self-confidence too early, so as not to give the gremlins of poetic justice too much of a field day in the event of things going wrong. And so the country will find it hard to forgive the young forward Raúl his pre-tournament indiscretion, when he carelessly quipped to a passing reporter that "I see myself as a world champion". Like David Beckham, he may pay with his soul for some time to come.

injustice for all

Norbert N. Ouendji

The record will show

that Cameroon departed the 1998 World Cup in much the same manner as they bowed out of USA 94, by finishing last in their first round group. In fact the Lions were only only outclassed once, in the 3-0 defeat by Italy, and had cause for cursing their luck.

Spirits had been high before the Italy match, with the independent newspaper *Le Messager* quoting the players' confident predictions of victory. The supporters, too, buoyed up by the team's good showing in the 1-1 draw against Austria, were expecting great things. The disillusion afterwards, therefore, was total. *Le Messager* wrote that the actor Daniel Ndo, father of defender Joseph Ndo, only just avoided "hitting his television in front of which he lay motionless and prostrate for several minutes".

According to the talk in the bars and cafes back home, the decisive moment came just before half-time when Kalla Nkongo received what was widely interpreted as a harsh red card. Roger Milla and

Joseph Antoine Bell, two famous Cameroon ex-internationals, held court in the local press, denouncing the management's tactics. The most common criticism was that François Omam Biyick, who had just had a bad season with Sampdoria and seemed to have been getting worse since the qualifiers, did not deserve a place in the starting line up. No one could understand, either, why coach Claude Le Roy continued to restrict Patrick Mboma, a born attacker and one of the top scorers in the J-League, to a defensive midfield role – the position that Marc Vivien Foé filled brilliantly until breaking his leg just before the start of the World Cup.

Despite the lesson given by the Azzuri, some fans still remained confident that Cameroon could qualify for the second phase by beating Chile on June 23rd. In the working class districts of the capital Yaoundé, and most of the other major towns, people crowded into bars, cafes, service stations, and anywhere with a television set, singing songs composed especially for the occasion. Even the 3,800 inmates in the central prison in Yaoundé were watching on the eight television sets provided by the authorities on match days. The prisoners in Douala, the business capital of the country, had the same privilege. Everyone felt involved.

Many supporters may still have believed they could have done a better job as national coach than Le Roy, but the changes he made in the line up met with general approval. Mboma rightly retook his place up front, and it was he who, in the 55th minute, equalised Sierra's opener for Chile, following a pass from Omam, who was playing astonishingly well compared to previous matches. The latter even scored a goal which the Hungarian referee Vagner disallowed, to the immense distress of the fans in the stadium, whose despair was caught by the cameras.

At the final whistle of a match that finished 1-1 and nine against 11, Song and Etame Mayer having been sent off, everyone was in uproar. The press was indignant. "It was the referee who knocked out the Indomitable Lions" said the state newspaper *Cameroon Tribune* the following day, while the players spoke of a victory being "stolen". A day later, the presenter of the morning sports programme on FM 94, an urban state-run radio station in Yaoundé, went even further, saying: "June 23rd 1998 should be remembered as the date of the biggest injustice ever suffered by the people of Cameroon."

Garga Haman Adji, president of the opposition Alliance pour la Democratie et le Developpement, released a press statement protesting about the performance of Mr Vagner, while *Le Messager* referred to a "deep feeling of frustration exacerbated by a fussy referee who robbed Cameroon of a victory that would have allowed them to continue in the competition".

In Yaoundé and Douala, white people's property was attacked and the police had to intervene to disperse the rioters. The violence ended with the death of a 17-year-old student, Ekouel Theophile, killed by the bullet of a policeman who, according to *Le Messager*, was trying to bring the incidents in Yaoundé "under control". It seems that Theophile was an innocent victim, given that the papers reported he was returning home from studying for an exam.

Didier Angibeaud, one of the revelations of France 98, who has since signed for Sturm Graz in Austria, claimed that the "anger of the people of Cameroon was understandable... but going on from there and attacking whites isn't right". The government appealed for calm. The Confédération Africaine de Football (CAF) and the Cameroon federation (FECAFOOT) contacted FIFA demanding compensation. The Minister for Youth and Sport, Joseph Owona, talked of a "conspiracy" against Africa; then decided to "cheer the players up" by paying them a "win bonus" – CF6 million each (approximately £6,000).

They spent their bonuses in different ways. Joseph Ndo bought a Toyota Carina for his father, as well as giving him money for improvements to the family home and to the stage school that he founded in Yaoundé. William Andem, one of the three goalkeepers in the squad, went to the prison in Douala to share his money with the prisoners. He gave them boxes of soap, sacks of rice and salt and a FIFA-approved football during a ceremony in the courtyard of the prison. "I chose the prisoners because I know that they are in need... just because we're satisfied doesn't mean that we should forget those who are suffering," Andem explained.

Other players spent a lot of money on parties before returning to the countries where they play their club football. Djanka Beaka, the scorer of the remarkable goal against Austria, and Joseph Ndo, the two first-choice players out of the four home-based players in the squad, will from now on make up part of this foreign legion. The newspapers revealed that they have been bought by Le Roy's new club, Strasbourg.

Amid all the praise, there were also some harsher analyses of the Lions' overall performance. Joseph-Antoine Bell, ex-goalkeeper of the national side and correspondent for Radio France Internationale (RFI) and the weekly magazine *France Football*, started the debate in an article published in *Le Messager* on July 3rd, underlining that "the refereeing alone cannot explain the elimination of the Indomitable Lions, who, even though they showed much courage and determination, nonetheless played far too cautiously". There was no advantage to be gained, Bell argued, in the Lions taking such a physical approach to the game, highlighted by the three red cards picked up during the tournament. According to Bell, the coach made no effort whatsoever to discipline his charges. "Claude Le Roy doesn't understand that physical intimidation is out of date," he claimed. "The laws of the game have been modified in such a way that violence no longer benefits its perpetrators."

Nonetheless, Le Roy and his management team received the same plaudits as the players on their arrival in Yaoundé on June 28th. They were received that night by the prime minister, Peter Mafany Musonge, along with government ministers and thousands massed in the streets. During his visit to the Lions before their match against Austria in Toulouse on June 11th, the head of state, Paul Biya, had even proposed to Le Roy that he become a special presidential advisor in sporting matters.

Several government officials had taken a keen interest in the World Cup, sometimes with dubious motives. Vincent Onana, president of FECAFOOT, was arrested before the tournament and imprisoned for his part in an illegal ticket distribution affair. The scam involved agents in England, where, the press reported, Onana had speculated for personal gain. The ministers for youth and culture led delegations of local artists and entertainers to France, though it turned out that some were not given tickets for the games. *Mutations*, a twice-weekly newspaper in Yaoundé, reported that the trip featured "a large number of sexual harassments", and added that on returning some of the performers had a "misunderstanding" with the minister of culture from whom they were expecting CF500,000 (£500) each for travelling expenses.

Several months on, and France 98 is still making headlines in Cameroon, where the minister for youth and sport and the FECAFOOT committee continue to fight for their share of the pot from France 98, a sum in excess of CF1 billion (£1 million). Hopefully it will be resolved before the start of the next World Cup campaign.

Translated from the French by Richard Guy

the righteous brothers

Andrew Jackson

My World Cup began

on the day Teddy Sheringham was caught out of school uniform in a Portuguese night club. He was upstaged in Denmark by Brian Laudrup confiding to the Danish media that he was looking forward to his team's stay in Provence, as it would give him a chance to check out one or two vineyards he had an interest in. Could any of England's squad have made that statement? Small consolation perhaps, after Laudrup Junior's subsequent resignation from international football at the the age of 29, but we should at least be able to look forward to an improvement in wine imports from France.

Watching the World Cup in Denmark was a mixed blessing. Denmark were in it, so at least the TV stations covered their matches, as well as a choice of obvious crowd-pleasing pairings involving mainly Brazil (whom everyone for some reason wanted to win) or Germany (whom everyone wanted to lose). Thank God for the sports-loving Swedes, who were not even in the thing, but still transmitted every match on one channel or other, regardless of the anti-football lobby.

Everyone in Denmark agreed that the two most boring first-round matches were England v Tunisia and Denmark v Saudi Arabia. Me too. We did get confirmation, however, of the precocious promise of Martin Jørgensen, whose mother revealed in a TV interview that little Martin used to hide under her dress during thunderstorms.

In the next match we got the mad Colombian referee, Señor Toro Rendon, who yellow-carded a South African player for time-wasting in the first half with his side 1-0 down. He also cautioned Peter Schmeichel for drawing attention to a substitution. Altogether seven yellows (South Africa won 4-3) and three reds (Denmark shaded this 2-1) in a match as innocent of dirty play as I can remember.

One German journalist said to a Danish colleague the next day that he was now able to understand why they shot referees in Colombia.The Danish press fell over each other to print pictures of Señor Toro Rendon taken from a worm's eye view so that he looked like a strutting Latin American military dictator. But, oddly enough, 1-1 was a fair result.

Denmark's last group match against France was a question of lambs to the slaughter. Had Denmark dared to do anything but lose, they would have incurred President Chirac's jowl-quivering rage as well as poor old Michel Platini's tears, so a quick dressing-room chat resulted in a decision to go for the second round tie with Nigeria, in preference to Denmark's bogey team Spain, fancied to come second in the "group of death". This required a calculated defeat at the hands of France, and a neat bit of hindsight on my part.

Some of us already thought Nigeria were over-rated, although it wasn't quite the done thing to say so. Teams from sub-Saharan Africa – but not the north African ones, for no discernible reason – enjoy a kind of idiotic media-induced popularity here, on a par with the "samba soccer" drivel written about Brazil.

Many people were saying that Michael Laudrup had outlived his usefulness to the team, as Denmark fielded a 4-5-1 formation with

Brian Laudrup alone up front. Still, they didn't have any other strikers of proven quality. Hindsight proves Denmark's coach Bo Johansson correct in keeping faith with the skipper in the later matches. Johansson has, incidentally, accomplished the previously impossible task of being both Swedish and popular in Denmark. He even speaks Danish, albeit with an accent, which is not something most Swedish immigrants in Denmark trouble themselves with, incorrectly assuming that we all understand them anyway.

The scripted defeat at the hands of France duly occurred. Vieira was lucky to finish on the pitch after a horrendous studs-first tackle on Schønberg's "groin area". Shortly before the end Schmeichel showed how anglicised he has become by clearing the ball out of the ground and signalling a six. But as it turned out Denmark didn't need to lose to France after all, as Paraguay pipped Spain for the second place in Group D.

A curious footnote was provided by Elton John, who gave a concert in Copenhagen the same night that England played Romania. As he re-emerged to do his first encore, he solemnly intoned "Colombia one, Tunisia nil. Romania two, England one. Still, we've got a hopeless manager. Man's an absolute prick." That's one potential employer Glenn can cross off his list. Ten minutes later Sir Elton emerged for a second encore wearing Denmark's kit. What a trouper.

So then, in the knock-out stage, Denmark's World Cup really started. Nigeria's coach Bora Milutinovic scored a PR own goal three days before the two sides met by saying he was concentrating on the quarter-final with Brazil. He then said the opposite the day after, warning his players against complacency. But the horse had bolted. Only Nigeria's captain, Uche Okechukwu, who used to play in front of Schmeichel for Brøndby and who is now a team-mate of Jes Høgh's in Fenerbahce, appeared to have heard of Denmark. Defender Taribo West was dismissive of Denmark's "British long ball style". Close, Taribo, but that must be Norway. Different place. Bit hillier, too.

I read some sniffy British reports of Denmark's stunning victory over Nigeria, and wondered what they would have said if England or Scotland had achieved the same result. A thrashing for MPlatini's other favourites, and it was done by swamping their midfield and counter-attacking, not, as you may have heard from misguided Brits, by the Nigerians having a collective off day. Their off day began after an hour when they saw the match finally going away from them with Michael Laudrup's amazing pass to Ebbe Sand for Denmark's third goal. The young Brøndby striker had been finding international football a little harder than the *Superliga* until Nigeria's defenders decided to give the lad's self-confidence a boost. His name is also a headline writer's dream, since it means not only "sand", but also "true" or "genuine". Hilarity was unconfined.

I watched the match with my friend Henning and his Dad. The Danish commentators were oddly subdued, as if they didn't believe what was happening. So were Henning and his Dad. I, the daft Englishman, compensated by leaping up and spilling beer at each goal. Peter Møller, whom nobody really rates, scored early, silencing his critics and provoking the German tabloid *Bild* into saying that he was "the biggest find of the World Cup" (who is this Michael Owen anyway?). Møller might not be the natural heir to the legendary Preben Elkjaer, but at a press conference he did a fine imperson-ation of Elkjaer, now a TV "expert", bemoaning Denmark's lack of quality strikers to play alongside his good self.

Bring on the Brazilians. Marc Rieper would take care of Ronaldo, and Dunga would wear himself out chasing Michael Laudrup's shadow. Or maybe not. In any event, this was the third time big brother would be playing his final match for his country. Denmark's quarter-final was arguably the best match of the tournament, although subsequently I couldn't find anyone in England who could remember watching it.

We might have had the upset of this or any World Cup tournament if Rieper's last-minute header had gone under the bar instead of hitting it, or if Schmeichel had not proved strangely vulnerable to long shots, prompting a few to wonder if perhaps he is over the hill. Zagallo said afterwards that his players were burnt up in the 90 minutes, and certainly Brazil were unimpressive in their semi-final against Holland, not to mention in the final itself. Clearly Denmark had softened them up.

I will not forget watching Michael Laudrup walking off the pitch after his final match as a professional player. Tears were shed. Brian Laudrup rather curiously refused to swap his shirt with any of his throng of Brazilian admirers, giving it to a Danish fan instead. Three days later we found out why, as he announced he would join his brother in international retirement. He hadn't wanted to make it known before the tournament, as Michael had done, because he wanted Michael to get the limelight.

Bo Johansson hopes he will change his mind, but I doubt it. the English media may surmise that he really wants to concentrate on keeping Chelsea in the Premiership, but don't believe a word of it. For one thing, Brian is devoted to his family. And the stress of being expected to be the match winner every time he pulls on the red shirt has finally got to him – although some of us wouldn't mind that kind of stress. Denmark will never replace the brothers, and if they were a Premiership side, they would already be relegation favourites. All of a sudden a European Championship group containing Italy, Switzerland, Belarus and Wales is looking a bit frightening.

Denmark's assistant coach, Flemming Serritslev, said that the Laudrup brothers were two of the finest people you could meet both on and off the pitch. The strange thing is that, despite my finely honed cynicism, I think he may be right.

clash of symbols

Dragomir Pop-Mitic

On May 29th,

Yugoslavia played their last home friendly before France 98, against Nigeria in front of a capacity crowd at the Red Star Belgrade stadium. For the first time in their history Yugoslavia played in dark blue shirts instead of traditional royal blue, for reasons which were never officially explained. The game finished in a predictably easy 3-0 win for the home side but, as usual in the modern Yugoslavia, an occasion which might have seemed tailor-made for fostering national unity was instead marred by division and confusion. It was a theme which was to characterise Yugoslavia's entire World Cup, albeit one with a surprisingly positive twist at the end.

Ever since the departure of Slovenia, Croatia, Bosnia and Macedonia from the federation, there has been strife over the national anthem and flag of Yugoslavia, which now consists only of Serbia and Montenegro. Many people prefer the old monarchist anthem (which has also been adopted by the Bosnian Serb statelet), while President Slobodan Milosevic's regime clings stubbornly to the old communist symbols. The result is that at least four different flags can be seen in the stadium when the national team plays, and there is a total boycott of the official anthem by the fans. Instead they sing the old anthem or simply boo. Red Star Belgrade supporters add their own famous chant: "Red Star, Serbia, never Yugoslavia."

So it was that in the match against Nigeria the anthem was howled down as usual. Nevertheless, the players themselves were more popular than ever, and unprecedented optimism over the team's chances in France was spreading around the country. Cries of "Dejo", to the tune of Harry Belafonte's *Banana Boat Song* rang out everywhere in tribute to Dejan Savicevic. "Dejo, you are a genius, you are God," went the national team's unofficial World Cup song.

Only a few people – unfortunately including the coach Slobodan Santrac – remained untouched by the mood of national euphoria. One newspaper ran a poll to find out who its readers least wanted to see in France. The lucky winners were Yugoslav president Slobodan Milosevic, Santrac himself and Savo Milosevic.

Shortly after the Nigeria game, Santrac decided that Albert Nadj (Real Betis) and Anto Drobnjak (Lens) would not go to France. The non-selection of Nadj was a particular surprise, but the football public were so confident about the ability of the key players that nobody worried too much. Even after poor performances against Switzerland (1-1) and Japan (1-0), the general secretary of the YFA, Branko Bulatovic, proclaimed: "Our main problem is that we have no problems." And we believed him.

Almost the only dark cloud on the horizon for the fans before the first game with Iran was the attitude of the national TV station, whose infuriating habit of inserting commercials into the middle of matches had caused the weekly magazine *Vremo* to call for a boycott of all goods advertised during the World Cup. The advertisements interrupted the game perpetually – when players were injured, when the ball went out for a corner or a throw-in, and sometimes also after a goal. While admittedly they were not quite as intrusive during the World Cup itself, they still managed to ruin the games as a spectacle.

Iran were unattractive and unkown opponents for most of the fans, and even some of the players. The best the coaching staff could come up with were platitudes: "there are no weak teams in the finals"; "they have some players in the Bundesliga"; "the opening game is always the hardest one". Despite the news that some players were doubtful with injuries, the only question seemed to be whether Yugoslavia could emulate their record 9-0 win over Zaire in 1974.

We knew something was wrong as soon as we heard Savo's voice during the playing of the national anthem: "They [the fans] are singing!" he said. The majority of Yugoslavia's supporters at the game were exiles who had left the country before the civil war and retained an emotional attachment to the old anthem. It was a discordant start to what turned out to be a nightmare game, from which Yugoslavia escaped thanks only to a feeble free-kick from Sinisa Mihailovic which the Iran keeper allowed to creep in.

No sooner was the game over than former national team player Stanislav Karasi was attacking Santrac and the players on TV. "Mijatovic is much more interested in promoting his new white boots than in scoring goals," he said. "I'm hoping for much better performances, because these players could not play worse than today." While Santrac's attempts to discuss the the tactics of the game were derided, the players were more honest. "We played like a village team," said Zeljko Petrovic.

The mood changed almost instantly. People started to talk about how much they had enjoyed watching the last World Cup and European Championship, when Yugoslavia were excluded because of the international sanctions imposed on them during the wars in Croatia and Bosnia. No pain, no tears, just drink and football. Ironic chants of "Bring back sanctions" began to make themselves heard.

Rumours began to circulate that all was not well among the players. Certainly their injury problems were all too real, and it suddenly seemed as though most of the starting XI were unfit. In particular, the numerous and mysterious injuries ascribed to Savicevic became a national joke, culminating in sarcastic headlines when he was stung by a bee.

The next match, however, was no joking matter. For most people in Yugoslavia, Germany looms large as a historical enemy rather than simply a rival in sport. "Let's beat the Germans, and after that we don't care," was a sentiment heard among many fans. The press also did their best to crank up an anti-German campaign. On the morning of the game the theme of the papers was: What the Germans have done to the Serbs this century. Their litany began with the World Cup defeats of 1954, 1958, 1974 and 1990. But no one hesitated to mention the First World War, the Second World War and all the other wars between the 1913 Balkan War and the latest one, during which the Germans always supported our enemies. Most prominent of all were reminders of the painful law imposed during 1941-45, when Serbia was occupied by the Germans and the fascist *Ustashe* regime ruled neighbouring Croatia: "For one dead German soldier, 100 Serbs have to be killed."

The determination of some of the players to provide "football war on the field" did little to calm the atmosphere. Both of Yugoslavia's goals were celebrated with flares and gunfire, and after the second one we were already world champions in the minds of many. Singing "*Auf Wiedersehen*" to German fans was something that generations of Yugoslav football fans could only dream about. Even in this game, however, the dream lasted only for 75 minutes.

Yugoslavia are used to throwing away big leads, but still it was hard to believe that a repeat of yet another debacle against the Germans – 1976 – was on the cards. That year in the European championship semi-final, Germany trailed 2-0 at half-time, only to end up 4-2 winners after extra-time, thanks to a Dieter Müller hat-trick. In the aftermath of the game in Lens, some commentators tried to persuade their audience that we outplayed the Germans, that we were a classy side full of skilful players, that it was a clash between physical strength and football skill – and finally, that we were very unlucky. The word "unlucky" was the last one anybody wanted to hear, because we were fed up of being unlucky, especially against the Germans. Yugoslavia did not know how to score that third goal, and no amount of bluster about being "moral winners" could change that. "In the dressing room we felt like we had lost the game," said goalkeeper Ivica Kralj. The nation felt the same.

Fortunately, the final group game was against the US. While basketball matches between the two countries have always been big events for Yugoslavia, the US is still regarded as a Mickey Mouse football nation. With the news that Savicevic and Mijatovic would finally play alongside each other, the mood reverted to the boundless hubris seen before the Iran game. **Repeat Of 1956?** asked one headline, recalling the only previous meeting between the two sides, when Yugoslavia won 9-1.

But the comedown also recalled what happened against Iran. After an early goal, we got a shock when Mijatovic went off injured in the 29th minute. For the next hour the players were uninterested in creating any decent opportunities, and just wanted to to avoid injury. Savicevic finally played for 25 minutes but did nothing, as did Savo, who, as one journalist put it, "played as though he was lost in space".

The official verdict was that the team had done a great job. The empty streets showed what the fans thought of another poor performance and the prize of a game against Holland. A couple of days after the match, the first sets of supporters started drifting back from France. They decided not to stay for the Holland game, because greedy officials from the YFA were selling the tickets on the black market at extremely high prices. The distribution of tickets for Yugoslav fans was shrouded in mystery throughout the tournament, alienating and frustrating many supporters who had spent a fortune just to get to France.

Over the weekend the injury news was encouraging, although after the tournament we found out that the bulletins were outright lies. Santrac promised that the most attacking formation would start the game. Yet when the TV coverage started it was immediately announced that he had discovered that Holland would start with six attacking players, and he had therefore opted to play 4-5-1.

Back home, we were speechless with horror at this choice of the unpopular formation known as "the bunker". Although Yugoslavia had chances to win, notably through Mijatovic's missed penalty, going out to a last-minute goal was somehow logical. Santrac refused to accept responsibility for a terrible performance. Worse, for many of the fans, he will always be remembered as the only person who opened his mouth during the playing of the anthem.

The first reactions after the game were as before. Yugoslavia put up a brave performance, but were undone by injuries, a bad referee, Bergkamp's stamping. The TV commentator smiled all the time and even made some jokes during his interview with Mijatovic and Santrac. He mentioned the Scottish fans, and their wonderful behaviour after the defeat by Morocco. But Yugoslav fans are not like that. We hate to lose games and we do not enjoy singing after defeats. Even President Milosevic sent a telegram to congratulate the team on their "dignified behaviour". But the next morning's papers were much more acceptable to the fans. **Bitter Taste Of Great Success** read one headline. "In the end we were humiliated and buried," said another commentator.

The next few days passed in sharp criticism of Santrac's work. The country was united in calling for his resignation, which was eventually forthcoming at the end of July. Members of his staff did not hesitate to weigh in with attacks on their boss, his training sessions ("more warm-ups than training") and his tactics. According to one journalist, the only winner of the last game was Savo Milosevic: "He did not play, he did not miss a penalty, and so he was not guilty of anything in that game."

Before the end of the tournament, a new song had already become popular, a losers' anthem with the refrain:

Fuck you footballers,
You play like amateurs

Yet, out of all this bitterness and disappointment, there was still something left in the tournament for Yugoslavia. Perhaps surprisingly for many people outside the country, it was called Croatia. Before they played Germany, the Croats were treated more or less the same as any other team in the tournament by the Yugoslav media. Their games were reported without much emotion. There was some low-key comment about Slaven Bilic's secret visit to the Yugoslav camp. Other articles mentioned that Davor Suker and some of his team-mates had supported Yugoslavia against Holland, and that many of the Yugoslav and Croatian players remained great friends (Suker and Mijatovic, for example).

But the game between Croatia and Germany brought about a whole new relationship between Yugoslav fans and the Croatian team. The Croats did something that our players had not been capable of. The newspapers lauded "the great, brave Croats, who absolutely deserved a famous victory". It was obvious that many fans were supporting Croatia during the game.

Although it was not altogether a surprise, the level of support for Croatia gave rise to a certain amount of theorising in the media. Among the reasons suggested were that five of the Croatian team (Suker, Jarni, Stimac, Boban and Prosinecki) had been part of the Yugoslav Under-20 team that beat Germany in the final of the World Youth Cup in 1988. That golden generation also included three of the current Yugoslavia squad (Mijatovic, Lekovic and Brnovic) and is still thought of with a great deal of affection throughout Yugoslavia.

Then there was the welcome development that Croatia did not overtly use their football success for political, anti-Serb provocation, as they had done at the basketball European Championships in 1995. There the Croatian players, who had won the bronze medal, refused to stay to see Yugoslavia lift the trophy. But this time there were no such incidents.

Perhaps harder to understand, in the light of the recent hostility between the two nations, is that the very nationalism of the Croats

also aroused admiration in Yugoslavia. Unlike our own players, they played unequivocally for the nation, for the national flag and the anthem, and they were motivated by a desire to promote the country. They gave the kind of performances we wanted to see from our own team.

The support for Croatia was genuine and arresting, although now, of course, we cannot wait to play them in the qualifiers for Euro 2000. Nor should it be thought that their success at the World Cup has done anything permanent to heal the breach between the two peoples. In August, Yugoslavia became basketball world champions, and our supporters at the finals in Greece did not forget either the footballers or the Croats in their chants:

Fuck you footballers!
Where are you now Ustashe?

island records

Anthony André

For any football fan

there is a defining moment in your life when you start to grow up and everything falls into place, a kind of sporting puberty. Offside suddenly makes sense and every player kicking against your beloved team isn't worth the shirt his name is printed on. From then on you gradually become enthralled, then totally wrapped up. For hundreds, maybe thousands of fans worldwide, that football awakening came on Sunday November 16th 1997, the day Jamaica qualified for the World Cup finals for the first time.

In the months before that, football fandom had become reasonably cool within the black community. That is not to say black people in general hadn't normally visited football grounds in Britain before – I had been going to Upton Park since my school days – but the Reggae Boyz experience changed many a perspective.

From the spring of 1997, whether you were Jamaican or not, the place to be seen was at one of the live satellite screenings of Jamaica's qualifying group matches, beamed straight into the heart of east London.

Some smart entrepreneur thought it would be a good idea to make it more of a fun social event. After all, everywhere else football was trendy. And in truth, despite a smattering of hard-core fans, for the majority of the viewers, this was the closest they had ever been to live football. Very few imagined that months later they would be contemplating making arrangements to see the same players in the World Cup.

Personally, I viewed the rise of the Reggae Boyz as some sort of sporting anomaly, a kind of footballing X-File. For reasons beyond my comprehension, everything about them was appealing – other than their style of football. Although I had visited Jamaica at least twice a year since 1994, I had no Jamaican ancestry to speak of, so my only excuse for pledging allegiance to the Reggae Boyz had to be the lame one that so many others would also use in the months to come – they were "the next best thing", the football equivalent of the West Indies cricket team. If Norman Tebbit had stopped me in the street and put me through his "who do you cheer for?" test, I would have failed miserably.

Although born in east London, I had lived and worked in the eastern Caribbean for six years and hankered for most things even remotely Caribbean. If I could find a place in my heart for someone like Dwight Yorke, who played for a side that sported claret and blue and wasn't West Ham, then supporting the Reggae Boyz was not such a great leap. Jamaica's qualification amazed me, since they were widely regarded as only the second-best team in the Caribbean region, behind six-times winners of the inter-island Shell Cup, Trinidad and Tobago. But with the islands being so small, not wanting Jamaica to progress could only seem like sour grapes.

In all previous World Cups it had been far easier for black fans to identify with the Brazilians, who had more black players in their side than any other nation, at least until the strides taken by Cameroon and Nigeria in the Nineties. Even a current England international such as Les Ferdinand has no qualms about having adopted Brazil as a child. It was simply what most Afro-Caribbean kids did.

For those of us now over 30, the tendency to look for teams other than England to support was exacerbated by the treatment given to the quality black players we grew up with. Perhaps we were biased, but it seemed to us that the likes of Cyrille Regis, Luther Blissett and Laurie Cunningham were never given a fair throw of the dice as far as international duty was concerned.

In 1982, Denis Alcapone's record *World Cup Football* made the case bluntly:

> *If England want to do some good*
> *Hear me now, hear me now Ron Greenwood*
> *Forget your pride and your prejudice*
> *And carry the man Cyrille Regis*
> *Get out your little notebook*
> *And write down the name Garth Crooks*

However, when players such as Viv Anderson and John Barnes became regulars in the side in the early Eighties it began to change many people's perception of the England set-up for the better. And while it still baffles me that Carlton Palmer ever got to sport those three lions on his shirt, having something or someone to identify with did wonders for those black fans who wanted to take their support beyond club level. Yet for many black British people support for England remained conditional and tentative, whereas the rise of Jamaican football satisfied all their cravings almost all at once.

The Reggae Boyz were first unleashed on London via satellite, with live match screenings staged in a small south London wine bar. At first word of mouth brought less than 100 weary weekend ravers out in the small hours to see footballers whom many had only read about in the local community press.

If the truth be known, the first time Jamaica really made the headlines on their World Cup trail was when fighting broke out during a friendly in Mexico in April 1997. Everyone with access to a satellite dish saw the fight footage flashed every half hour on Sky News. While the tone of the news package suggested strongly that Jamaican football wasn't to be taken too seriously, it raised public awareness. Until then, not too many people had even realised that the island side had a chance of World Cup qualification. When the news broke that, as a result of the Mexico brawl, there was a slim possibility that they would be banned by FIFA from taking any further part, their stock rose even further.

Later that month those qualification hopes seemed to have disappeared in any case, as the Jamaicans were thrashed 6-0 by Mexico. Yet the screenings continued and the fan base grew stronger. Caribbean football was providing a night out on a par with any post-concert party. Weeks later, the introduction of British-born players aroused the interest of more of the as yet unconverted, although it was still viewed more as a curio when Paul Hall – then of First Division Portsmouth – and his team-mate Fitzroy Simpson, along with Derby's Deon Burton and Wimbledon's Robbie Earle, joined the Jamaican set-up.

Their influence proved to be phenomenal, both on the side's fortunes and for the business-minded promoter who initiated the live satellite screenings. He was forced to move to the much larger east London home of boxing, York Hall in Bethnal Green, as more and more people fell under the spell of the Reggae Boyz. The atmosphere was unbelievable. A handful of avid football fans had grown into a swarm of anxious individuals all hoping for the same thing – an excuse to party in the name of football.

While that motive may have been simple, the ties that bound the Jamaican team to London's black community were not. For the island side was drawing support not only from British-born people of Jamaican descent, but also from black people whose roots were in other parts of the Caribbean, traditionally hostile to domination by Jamaica in inter-island affairs. It was Jamaica's independence in 1961 that broke up the original short-lived West Indies Federation, and attempts to recreate something similar among the Commonwealth islands failed miserably in the 1970s. Now football seemed to have achieved at least a temporary unity.

A 0-0 draw against Mexico in November secured Jamaica a place at France 98, and from then until June Jamaica became the topic of practically every other conversation. People you hardly knew, and people you were sure hadn't the remotest interest in football, were suddenly engaging you in conversations about the merits of playing a home-grown side, and why the introduction of freeloading "Ja-fakens" would only lead to unrest and the island side's ultimate failure in France.

It was announced that the Reggae Boyz would tour the UK, and even an encounter with England was briefly mooted. David Mellor doubted whether Jamaican could muster enough support to fill Wembley, but even he could not have failed to warm to the atmosphere at Loftus Road as Jamaica took on QPR. Passion, joy and all the emotions you'd expect from a hippie love and peace rally or a Caribbean beach party filled the air. True, the team looked piss poor against a mediocre First Division outfit, but to the 16,000 supporters of Jamaica who had gathered, it didn't really matter.

And so to France. After so many months on the Jamaica World Cup trail, I could still recognise some of the faces in the crowd from earlier games and the east London satellite screenings a year previously. The high level of anticipation they brought with them to France petered out somewhat after the 3-1 defeat by Croatia, but a new and more inter-esting attitude began to take hold.

Until then not too many of my fellow Jamaican supporters had looked at the game as one that was actually being played to win – now they started to analyse and criticise the way they would with any other sporting performance. Prior to the defeat by Croatia the taking part was more important than the competing, but that game showed that the side need not necessarily be outclassed. But for a few tactical mistakes – like playing injured defender Frank Sinclair and clearly unfit midfielder Peter Cargill – the Reggae Boyz might have escaped with a draw against the eventual semi-finalists.

Like everyone else, I was intent on enjoying the Reggae Boyz for as long as they would last, which, based on everything I'd seen, read and knew about them, wouldn't be long. The bubble finally burst when Derby's Darryl Powell got himself sent off seconds before half-time against Argentina, prompting a second-half collapse and a 5-0 hammering. By then it was clear Jamaica's flirtation with world football

had come to an abrupt end, and even the fans knew it. Many had made the journey to Paris that day and would have seen a Channel 4 documentary exposé the night before. It did not present the English-based players in a good light and reportedly caused ructions in the team camp.

For perhaps the first time since the Mexico fight, community newspapers – the *Voice* included – laid into the team. First, they blamed the film and its producers for presenting a certain member of the English contingent in a way which would only exacerbate an already tense situation between the English-born and island-based players. Second, they blamed island footballing chiefs for their naiveté in granting a film crew unlimited access to the team. Third, they blamed the team for losing sight of what they had come to France to do. Needless to say there were no prolonged street celebrations in Paris after the Argentina game – as there had been after the Croatia defeat – as even the fans sensed something was wrong.

But if things began to fall apart in the training camp, the victory over Japan at least ended the tournament on a positive note. Regardless of the ups and downs, I doubt very much that any one of Jamaica's fans felt let down by the World Cup experience. I for one found the past year to be more than just one of those defining footballing moments. It was not so much a footballing puberty as a footballing coming of age experience, a road to Damascus by way of Jamaica.

then fall, Cesare

Roberto Gotta

Cesare Maldini's dismissal

provided the fitting ending to six crazy weeks in Italian football. The World Cup was, as usual, a carnival of controversy. While no one was vilified in quite the same manner as David Beckham for the team's failure to advance past the quarter-finals, the media was provided with enough ammunition for near 24-hour coverage.

Press coverage of Italian football is suffocating in normal times, so it is easy to imagine how things can get out of hand when it comes to a momentous occasion such as a World Cup. Early in the tournament criticism was directed at the state television network (RAI) for sending a disproportionately large number of people to France, though at the first outcry about the wasting of public money it was pointed out that the Italians had fewer technicians, journalists and assorted hangers-on than the BBC. No one bothered to check if that was true, and the whole controversy lasted only a few hours – perhaps not surprisingly, since most reporters' critical faculties were dulled by the fact that they were also living lavishly in France, at their newspapers' expense, not to mention appearing frequently as guests on RAI's programmes.

The sports dailies in particular sent hordes of reporters, in order to make sure that no possible angle remained uncovered. This obviously resulted in too many angles being covered, the obsession with details obscuring the real stories and making it hard for the viewer to see the wood for the trees. Their main campaign, even before the tournament started, was for Roberto Baggio to be included in the starting line-up, as Alessandro del Piero was struggling to recover from an injury sustained playing for Juventus in their Champions Cup final defeat by Real Madrid. After Baggio started, and played well, in Italy's first match against Chile, the focus shifted again: how could Maldini leave Baggio out now, but fit Del Piero in alongside him? The former Divine Ponytail made all the right noises about being a team player and knowing from the start that he was only standing in for Del Piero, but of course no one believed him.

If any proof were needed of the depths of the controversy, it was surely the sight of Maldini Senior arguing with fans in the stand during the match against Norway, when the clueless Del Piero was on the pitch for 77 minutes while Baggio stewed on the bench. "It's none of your business," was Maldini's memorable reply to the questions about his tactical decision. Peace of mind and of soul, you see, are not characteristic of Italian football during big events.

The critics held their fire after the lucky win over Norway, but when Maldini once again went for Del Piero in the game against France that saw Italy's elimination on penalties, the knives were out. Most of the commentators' post mortems focused on Italy's reluctance to take the game to France, their apparent will to hold on for a goalless draw then win on penalties, although others argued that Maldini's boys had been successful in stifling the home team's attacks and could have won with a little more luck. **No, Not Like This** was the sports daily *Tuttosport*'s headline (next to it was **AC Milan**

Offer £30m For Owen), while *Corriere dello Sport* screamed **Damn Penalties... But It's Also Our Fault**.

The most direct attack came from respected columnist Giorgio Tosatti, who, in his dual role as TV pundit for RAI's flagship *Occhio al Mondiale* (Eye on the World Cup) and chief commentator for *Corriere della Sera*, heavily criticised Maldini for his team's negative approach: "If we want Italy to play in another way," he wrote, "Maldini cannot stay in the job."

Few commentators cared to recall that two years ago Maldini's appointment was so popular it was almost greeted by street celebrations. That was partly due to his success in winning a few titles with Italy's Under-21 teams, but mostly to the fact that he replaced the hated Arrigo Sacchi, whose manic stare during tense moments on the sidelines is still causing nightmares to a generation of Italian schoolchildren.

At first, Maldini could do nothing wrong: his prudent tactical approach seemed perfect, after Sacchi's idiosyncratic, but increasingly ineffective attacking football. Maldini's down-to-earth personality also endeared him to many. No one really cared that he could barely speak comprehensible Italian, nor that he blatantly dyed his hair: he was everybody's favourite uncle, the quietly confident old sage as opposed to the obsessive parvenu. Italy's 1-0 win at Wembley in the qualifiers for France 98 continued Maldini's honeymoon, while Sacchi's futile attempts to rescue Milan from their plight were mocked by his enemies in the media.

But Italy's failure to win in Georgia and the subsequent home draw against England in the final qualifying match planted the first seeds of doubt. During the last few months of his tenure, and especially during the World Cup, Maldini increasingly came under fire for his defensive, risk-free outlook, even though this was the same approach that had earned him everybody's acclaim in the first place. Now, suddenly, he had to go.

"So long, Cesare" wrote *Il Giornale*'s Enzo Bucchioni after the team returned home (thankfully without a welcoming party of fans armed with sackfuls of tomatoes and rotten eggs, as had famously happened after the loss to North Korea in 1966). For Maldini, however, there was little respite. One sports daily pursued him to a beach in Tuscany, where they helpfully interviewed a 14-year-old boy who happened to have rented an umbrella and recliner next to Cesare's.

The more thoughtful and less populist sections of the press (hard to find, but they do exist) came to Maldini's defence, insisting that he had done as good a job as possible, given that he had been handed the reins almost overnight after Sacchi's "escape", that this was not a particularly talented squad and that he had never promised his team would be spectacular and exciting to watch. Chief counsel for the defence was *Tuttosport*, which, being Turin-based and Juventus-oriented, also took time out to point out that Del Piero's poor *Mondiale* wasn't really Alessandro's fault.

The arguments raging over Maldini were, of course, only the pinnacle of a vast mountain of media comment. With so many pages to fill, so many hours of airtime to use, it requires a very deep-thinking, forward-looking sports editor to create something new or especially interesting. One way, of course, would be simply to reduce the coverage, but that seems of out the question. In fact, with digital TV and the proliferation of magazines and internet sites, it seems certain that things will only get worse.

Between them, RAI's three channels and Telemontecarlo – owned by Fiorentina president Vittorio Cecchi Gori – broadcast something on the World Cup every hour of the day. Such overkill led to spectacles such as full morning re-runs of the previous day's matches (a practice which continued deep into July) and an avalanche of studio shows and location reports, which even included a woman reporter strolling around the Italian team's headquarters and interviewing empty chairs (don't ask).

The top show was *Occhio al Mondiale*, broadcast each day at 11pm. Its cast made for compulsive viewing: the aforementioned Tosatti, his TV colleague Giampiero Galeazzi and presenter Antonella

Clerici. Galeazzi, whose massive bulk increases year by year, is best known for his manic, passionate, screaming commentaries on men's rowing, a sport in which he took part years ago. He is a football and tennis expert, a closet Lazio fan and a presenter of the very popular *Novantesimo Minuto* (90th Minute), the programme which shows the day's goals for the first time (of many) at 6pm each Sunday during the domestic season. He was also notorious for pretending to shoot a live seal while dressed in a cowboy outfit on the Sunday afternoon family show which precedes *Novantesimo Minuto*. The seal, memorably, spat at him.

So *Occhio al Mondiale* promised much, but it delivered little. The hosts did their best, but Clerici had her work cut out to pry anything interesting from the lips of the guests, who usually included a journalist, an actress (the more she showed of her legs, the better her chances of being invited back, it seemed), and some strange characters who sometimes looked as if they had been just pulled from the street. The actress would invariably say a) she had been a football fan all her life, b) she was dating a footballer, or c) she didn't know anything about football, but it was fun being a guest anyway. After a full day of hearing serious, boring journalists analysing every last detail of Cesare Maldini's interviews, this was at least light relief. And a perfect send-off for those who had to go to sleep.

The public, on the whole, seemed to prefer *Da Parigi a Milano* (From Paris to Milan). The studio was in Paris, but the mention of Milan in the title referred to a terrifying feature of the show – the daily announcements of big deals and signings made by Italian clubs. The programme became universally regarded as unreliable after claiming an incredible number of scoops, which they divided into three categories: *bombette*, *bombe* and *superbombe* (little bombs, bombs, superbombs) – a bomb being a particularly succulent, you-heard-it-here-first story.

Anyone who actually kept tabs on the number of accurate "scoops" they obtained would have had trouble reaching double figures, but then the whole point of the programme was simply to be on the air

and make as much noise as possible – it was not uncommon for three guests to be speaking simultaneously, or even better, screaming at the top of their voices. That the dismal *Da Parigi a Milano* recorded significant ratings during the tournament is proof that Italians are partial to their controversies and aren't always too particular about the facts.

It would be completely wrong to give the impression that Italy did not take the World Cup seriously. However, in addition to the obsession with trivia and the mounting criticism of Maldini, a third factor conspired to undermine any sense of national unity generated by the performances of the *Azzuri*. Even as the fans were cruising the streets, honking their horns and waving flags after the epic win over, er, Cameroon, it was clear that once again a significant minority of them based their feelings toward the national team on which players from their club were represented. So some Inter fans were also rooting for Brazil (Ronaldo), France (Djorkaeff), Argentina (Zanetti) and so on.

One Juventus fan wrote to a newspaper urging Maldini to drop Del Piero. That way, he reasoned, Juventus would have no players in the Italian team and he would be free to hate them. Laughable as it was, it reflected an attitude of many: support your players first, then the national team, and if it wins, jump in your car, honk you horns, wave your flag and say "I always said we were going to win". I did not hear many car horns after France beat Italy. Maybe many were still stunned, others quietly grieving. And it was raining, after all.

A few weeks after the end of the tournament came the big news – goalkeeping legend Dino Zoff had been named as Maldini's replacement. Zoff was badly treated by Juventus, who fired him a few years ago in order to enter the stream of "new football" by hiring innovative, attacking football guru Gigi Maifredi, who lasted all of a season. Since then, Zoff had been with Lazio, being gradually promoted from coach to president.

His appointment can be considered an immediate effect of the World Cup, but the few fans who can actually think past each day's screaming headlines are already wondering. Zoff's football philosophy is not much different from Maldini's, and both share a curious reluctance to accept that the passing of time can make one's hair turn naturally grey. Stay tuned, then. If the pressure of managing Italy turns out to be as bad as it seems, Big Dino is going to have to spend a fortune in hair dye.

hope for the worst

Robin McMillan

A funny thing happened

on the way to San Francisco. After a four-hour flight from New York spent with knees wedged firmly in sternum, I hopped off during a stop-over in Dallas to stretch my legs and perhaps grab a quick cold one. It was June 15th, just before midday. Emerging from the gate, I noticed something odd. The concourse television monitors that usually air CNN – it's almost a federal regulation – were showing the World Cup. Romania against Colombia.

Off to the bar. Here, the televisions that usually show basketball, baseball, highlights of the previous day's sports action, or a couple of buff babes aerobicising, were also showing the World Cup. What was going on? Had a secret FIFA satellite blacked out all the other television channels? Had Nike taken over Dallas-Fort Worth? (They do airports, don't they?) Or was America finally aligning itself with the rest of the world and tuning into every last red card, red hair-do, and red herring of France 98?

Clearly, something was afoot. Eight years earlier, hardly a soul knew that the US had qualified for their first World Cup finals since 1950. Three losses and home, and everyone looked the other way. Four years later, the US hosted the World Cup, and put on something of a show, both in terms of organisation and in achievement. A solid, if unspectacular team reached the second round only to lose on July 4th, to Brazil. People took notice.

Now there were new factors to consider: a full-time professional league; new television channels that craved programming; success in the CONCACAF Gold Cup. All adding up to... to what? A blip on the radar screen? A steady rise in interest? A nation of ravenous soccer sluts?

It's a tough question to answer, because first we have to say what we mean by the United States. Do we mean the so-called "ethnic" population, those who already had a love for football and followed the World Cup through the fortunes of the lands of their fathers and grandfathers? These are the Brazilians who turn West 46th Street in New York City into one big block party, the Italians who unfurl flags all over the North Beach area of San Francisco, the Mexicans who turn Los Angeles into a ghost town when the *Aztecas* play. As columnist Bruce Jenkins wrote in the *San Francisco Chronicle*, "The games should be on all day, every day, in a dozen different languages. You'd be amazed how many people care."

Or perhaps we mean the "American" soccer fan, kids and younger adults who have grown up playing football and care about the US team. Or do we mean World Cup watchers – not to be confused with soccer watchers – who follow the other big US sports, but add the tournament to their sporting menus? Indeed, there is a solid argument that it is this group that contributes the most to any increase in interest around World Cup time.

There were several indicators that interest had grown substantially since 1994. Take the print media. Four years ago, Alexi Lalas was asked when soccer would succeed in the US. "When all the old sportswriters die," he replied. Well, the old ones may not be dead yet, but their younger counterparts seem to see soccer on its merits, and not as a threat to the big four (baseball, basketball, football and ice hockey). Where the World Cup once made the "In Brief" items and perhaps an occasional column, now some papers devoted entire sections to it. *USA Today* allowed at least one page per issue this time around. Ditto the *New York Times*. And the commentary was serious, too.

On June 20th, for example, the *Dallas Morning News* previewed Belgium-Mexico, Holland-South Korea and Croatia-Japan, with a map of the world pin-pointing each country, a rundown of each team's chances and the consequences of each possible result. Then there were television schedules and several news stories. That stuff didn't appear two World Cups ago, and, were it not for the fact that the US were the hosts in 1994, probably would not have appeared one World Cup ago.

Television, of course, remains the principal measure of success, because he who has a television contract usually wins (or at least has a chance of success). It was a lack of one that killed the NASL, and it is only because of its current one that Major League Soccer continues to exist. France 98 had unprecedented coverage. Every single match was aired in English, divided up between ABC and the two main cable channels, ESPN and ESPN2. Most nights also saw a replay of the best match of that day. In addition, the Spanish-language station Univision carried everything.

And did anyone watch? Sort of. ESPN had an average rating of around 1.0, while ESPN2 was about half that. A rating of 1.0 is equivalent to an audience roughly 40 times smaller than that for a prime-time episode of *Seinfeld*. But the midweek games aired at 11am and 2.30pm, when most people were at work. And no one heard ESPN complaining. The numbers were as good or better than the channels would have fetched had they aired their normal programming – in some cases they tripled their audience – and they weren't very far behind the Stanley Cup hockey finals. ABC drew several points higher for their prime-time weekend afternoon broadcasts.

Univision, on the other hand, outdrew ESPN and ESPN2 for almost every game (and set a record for the final), leading many to draw the obvious conclusion that soccer is still a game for the "ethnic" market. Not so fast. Although it hasn't been measured, the Univision broadcasts attract a lot of non-Spanish-speaking viewers, because the English-language commentators are so bad. Where such American "experts" as Rick Davis and Ty Keough drone on about tactics, sometimes ignoring the action, the Univision commentary reflects the drama and momentum of games. It didn't hurt either, of course, that Mexico, Argentina, Chile, and Paraguay made it past the group stage.

The net result was that you could ask just about anyone if they were aware that the World Cup was going on, and they would assure you that it was. Which is pretty impressive given the fierce competition at this time of year. There were the NBA basketball play-offs starring Michael Jordan; Major League Baseball starring the red-hot New York Yankees; US Open golf starring Tiger Woods; the Stanley Cup finals starring some big toothless goons from Canada; Triple Crown horse racing starring a lot of galloping horses; and Wimbledon, starring no one of any importance on this side of the pond.

How am I able to discern this interest? Because I asked people about it, in restaurants, on the subway, on planes, in airports, in several places in Manhattan, in taxis, around the office – although there it was my colleagues who brought it up first. One American writer friend who is interested primarily in baseball and golf called me every other day with a bunch of questions. "Why don't referees call shirt-pulling?" "What's wrong with our midfield?" "Who is this kid Owen?"

Three things happened to the US before the finals that were to have a great effect on their fortunes in France. The first was the defeat of Brazil in the Gold Cup. Granted, the Brazilians weren't at full strength, but Kasey Keller was terrific and, well, it was Brazil. Confidence soared. Second, John Harkes was booted off the squad.

Coach Steve Sampson – who had made Harkes "captain for life" not so long before – said it was because of discipline and leadership problems, and that it was time to bring in new blood. But you had to wonder whether a temporary benching might have been a solution to the former, and whether the final stages of the World Cup was the ideal time for the latter.

Then the rumour mill got going. Nothing was ever substantiated, but Harkes was said to have:

1. Slept with a team-mate's wife
2. Slept with several team-mates' wives
3. Slept with Sampson's wife

At any rate, Harkes was sent to his room without any ice cream. Claudio Reyna, young and promising, but lacking Harkes's physical presence, was installed by Sampson as the playmaker. Confidence plummeted.

The third thing that happened was that the US beat Austria 3-0 in a friendly, in Austria. Playing somewhere in the middle of a relatively new 3-6-1 formation, Reyna scored one and made two. Suddenly, Sampson was correct, but you wanted to shout: "Steve, no! He's a little guy. You've left behind the big guy who should have been next to him! And it was a friendly! And he plays for – hang on while I look it up – Wolfsburg! The Germans will kill him!" Too late. Confidence soared once more.

So there was something of a soap opera going on as the US began their campaign against Germany. Top player left at home. Untested midfield general. New tactical system. An almost impossible draw. And a heap of folks whistling in the graveyard.

And what happened? Reyna is fouled early and is never heard from again. Germany score two soft goals, Dooley misjudging a cross and the entire US defence letting a header sneak in at the near post. Frankie Hejduk comes on in the second half wearing his shorts backwards in the hope that this will rally his team-mates.

Baseball players do it with their caps, and you know what? It doesn't work for them either.

After the game, Sampson and his players start snapping at each other. Sampson claims the players' criticism of his selections (or non-selections) is healthy, that it shows passion. To quote my 10-year-old: "Hello-o-o-o-o!"

Things get worse against Iran, who go ahead as Tab Ramos and Reyna are caught sightseeing and Zarincheh heads home the opener. The US press for an equaliser, hitting the woodwork several times, but succeed only in losing a second goal on the counter-attack. They do get one back, Brian McBride scoring with four minutes to go. Strange move: Sampson plays Roy Wegerle and benches Eric Wynalda, ineffective so far, yet still the team's top scorer. Then, when down 1-0 in the second half, he brings on defensive midfielder Brian Maisonneuve as Wynalda continues to ride the pine.

The tension between Sampson and his players is now palpable. Veterans such as Lalas and Marcelo Balboa are fuming that they have been cast aside. "There is a spirit that exists with this team that was there in the locker room and on the field, and it produced results," Lalas says. "That spirit has been carried by the guys who have grown up with the national team and who have had their lives changed as a result of our involvement with it. That spirit is missing right now."

A similar spirit is all too evident among the victorious Iranians, however. "Tonight again, the strong and arrogant nation felt the bitter taste of defeat at your hands," their government tells the team. "Be happy that you have made the Iranian nation happy." Over the top, perhaps, but it is easy to imagine what the reaction here would have been had the US won.

After succumbing to a third defeat against a patchy Yugoslavia side, it was only a matter of time before Sampson stepped down. The situation wasn't helped by the announcement that the US officially finished dead last in the tournament. In the days that followed, full-blown verbal battles broke out. Sampson skewered Tab Ramos for criticising his team selection, pointing out that this was a rich way to thank him for keeping his spot open for months, while he recovered from injury.

To try to put a bright spin on things, US soccer head Alan Rothenberg announced Project 2010, under which the US plan to reach the second round by 2002, the semi-finals by 2006 and to win it all in 2010. Which is to say that in the space of 12 years, the US will go from the worst in the finals to the best. And he was serious.

But if the performance of the team in France gave little grounds for optimism, there was some solid and anecdotal evidence that the World Cup is gradually securing a firmer hold in the American public's imagination. From sandwich shops in North Carolina to the streets of New York City, I heard of encouraging tales of interest and enthusiasm among sections of the population previously untouched by the soccer bug. A greater interest in the World Cup, or the national team, doesn't necessarily translate to support for the game as a whole, of course, although it can't hurt. The dozen or so colleagues of mine who stood at our office TV looking at "ITA" vs "CHI" and wondering why Italy were playing Chicago, were there partly because they had been through 1994.

And it's hard to be totally pessimistic about the future when the tournament inspired pockets of outright celebration as well as wide-ranging curiosity. The mother of a teenager I know told me how her son had watched the final wearing a Zidane jersey his coach had given him: "As he walked home through Soho [in Manhattan] people kept yelling 'Yeah, Zidane!!!' He got so-o-o-o much attention with that jersey and felt so proud. And Soho was wild. People were dancing and yelling and partying in the streets, with Brazilians on one side of the street and Frenchies on the other. What a wild day."

On to 2002. Wherever that may be.

Thanks to David Hershey, Steven Saltzman, Emery Benedek, Alex Chater, Michael and Brendan Moylan, Karen and Andrew Booth

fighting talk

Rutger Slagter

"Dutch players will only perform with 90 per cent of their capabilities if they think that is sufficient. In order to win the World Cup you need 100 per cent. They need to create something in order to get the players focused. A small row is necessary to be a great team rather than merely a good one." That was the opinion of Johan Cruyff, the father of the conflict model, before the start of France 98.

Without wishing to be blasphemous, it is fair to point out that during Euro 96 Edgar Davids "created something", just before the rest of the squad followed him home. The Dutch camps at the last two World Cups also caused enough problems among themselves to easily become world champions according to the Cruyff formula, yet somehow ended up without the silverware. Therefore the awkward silence that descended over the squad on the road to France eased a lot of nerves back home. Maybe it was time for something new, instead of the traditional "own worst enemy" performance.

Belgium's coach Georges Leekens, however, seemed to agree with the foreign media. "It's a shame we don't play Holland in the third match," he said. "When the Dutch have been together for two weeks there will probably be a problem again." On the other hand, he also said: "We are obliged to attack, because our qualities are up front." So perhaps his views should not be taken too seriously.

On the Dutch side, too, only a few of the 15 million coaches knew their football history. Since qualifying for Euro 88, Holland had been disappointing in their opening match of every tournament. The next five had produced two narrow escapes, two draws and a defeat. This time, too, the realists were proven right.

People joining the match late might have got the wrong impression from seeing the Belgian players celebrating with their fans and the coach smiling from ear to ear. Belgium's papers the next day carried headlines such as **Really Deserved** and **How Quiet Are The Dutch**. The Dutch press were more realistic. **Nervous Start** and **Belgium: Red Card** they proclaimed. Such restrained hostility is not untypical of relationships between the two countries. In Holland, whenever somebody makes a joke about a stupid person, the victim is normally a Belgian. Whereas the Belgians tend to think the Dutch are arrogant, and call them "fatnecks".

In the old days, when the two countries played little more than one match a year, and that against each other, the rivalry of ignorant v arrogant was a truly bitter one. But when more countries came on the scene, and especially since the footballing fortunes of Holland and Belgium diverged in the 1970s, the rivalry has taken something of a back seat. For Holland, at least, playing Belgium has been much less significant (as well as much less historically charged) than their clashes with Germany since 1974. Whatever the reaction of the two camps this time around, the fact was, from a neutral point of view, the match was well worth tuning in late for.

The natural high after Holland's easy win over South Korea in their second match was short lived. Wim Jonk's best friend died in a car crash a few days later. Should he play against Mexico or should he stay? Jonk wrote a poem for his friend and decided to stay.

In the run-up to the final group game there was again a lot of discussion about our neighbours. Why not draw with the Mexicans and see what happens to Lorenzo Staelens (who had got Patrick Kluivert sent off in the first game) and his friends? After 20 minutes, with Holland two up through Cocu and Ronald de Boer, it looked unlikely that Guus Hiddink had the same scenario in mind. At the same time, Luc Nilis scored against South Korea and Belgium were virtually through to the second round. A fax came through from the Belgian FA to the media centres: "There are no tickets available for the second round game of the Belgian squad." Then South Korea equalised, the Mexicans behaved disconcertingly like Germans, scoring twice in the last 15 minutes, and Staelens was home before his postcards.

Holland must be the only country in the world in which everyone is critical even when they win their group. The loss of concentration in the last part of the Mexico match was a cause for concern, and Jaap Stam, the most expensive defender in the world, looked like an amateur. Pundit Jan Mulder made his only sensible remark of the tournament: "Although he costs 35 million guilders, he should not try to play like Ronaldo." Cruyff, meanwhile, had Dennis Bergkamp in his sights. "What Dennis did was far below zero," he said. "I hope he shows some of his skills in the next match, and that goes for the rest of the squad too."

As always, the Dutch players listened to Him. Against Yugoslavia they dominated for all but ten minutes, and after Predrag Mijatovic, the penalty specialist whom Hiddink had brought to Valencia years before, had missed from the spot, the Dutch knew they would win. It was the first World Cup penalty missed in 37 attempts, excluding shoot-outs.

Cruyff, naturally, was still not enthusiastic. "Too much went wrong, tactically they were not good enough and it was striking how moderate the passing of Davids and Seedorf was," he said. Although presumably he was happy enough with the result. However, it was not the result that got the attention in the international media.

back
HOME

During the celebrations after the final whistle, Edwin van der Sar punched Winston Bogarde. A white player and a black player in a fight! It had taken a while, but finally there was trouble in the Dutch camp.

On Belgian TV the incident was replayed dozens of times. But the foreign journalists were disappointed after hearing the real story. The keeper was in the middle of the celebrations when somebody put an arm around his neck. "I couldn't breathe, panicked and had to free myself," Van der Sar said. Bogarde, who always celebrates in a fairly extravagant manner and looks like someone who could easily strangle you, was the obvious suspect. But in fact Pierre van Hooijdonk was the "guilty" party. Everything was immediately explained by the main characters, there were apologies all round and in Holland, at least, it was no big deal.

The next day, all the pundits and most players voted for England as their preferred next opponents. That is, until England's match against Argentina started. After 20 minutes there were doubts, at half-time everyone was sure: why not avoid England and get revenge for 1978, rather than 1996? A match-up with Argentina would even have an extra dimension, since coach Daniel Passarella was the captain of Argentina when they defeated Holland in the final 20 years previously, and he did not make many friends back then. Dutch assistant coach Johan Neeskens also played in the battle of Buenos Aires. Most of the 1978 squad had their say about the game, some even had tickets. Jan Poortvliet walked around in his shirt and shorts from the final. He would not be disappointed.

In the last minute, with the score 1-1, Bergkamp came up with his wonder goal and Holland exploded. The same people who had begged Hiddink to substitute him only seconds earlier were chanting his names in the streets and bars. The scenes called to mind the victories of Euro 88, and even the liberation at the end of the Second World War. A great day was made even better by Croatia beating Germany, although most Dutch people only realised this the next day, thanks to the combination of the excitement of the

Argentina game, and alcohol. While losing in 1978 was traumatic, the defeat of Holland's greatest ever team in the 1974 final by their German hosts rankles still further, even for people born after the game. Most Dutch fans have to stop the video and rewind after the first two minutes of that match.

For the players, however, there was little time to celebrate, especially since Holland were the only team in the last four with only three days between matches. After a tournament in which memories of 1974 and 1978 were at least softened, if not exorcised, a third final against the host nation was nevertheless not to be. When Kluivert missed by centimetres in extra time, most Dutch fans realised it was over, since Holland's recent shoot-out record is little better than England's (defeats against Denmark at Euro 92 and France at Euro 96).

L'Equipe concluded: **Orange Dominated, But Taffarel Was The Hero**. Platini added that he thought it was Holland who brought flavour to the World Cup, but that was little consolation to players or fans. This should have been the year. After the tournament Edgar Davids, who would not have been in the first five before the matches started, was voted Holland's most popular player. He will be there in 2002 to try again. Whether Bergkamp, the fans' second choice, will join him seems unlikely. As Hiddink explained, "it's a long way through Asia by car". Hiddink himself probably will not be there either, after signing for Real Madrid. Most of the prominent Dutch coaches were named in connection with the national team job, one in particular, before the eventual appointment of Frank Rijkaard. Maybe now we will never know what Cruyff would have created to get the players focused.

changing of
the guard

Jeremy Lennard

It is never a good sign

when your team's goalkeeper is crowned the star of a tournament, and when Colombia's weepy No 1 Farid Mondragón was elevated to hero status after the team's first game – their 0-1 defeat against Romania – it seemed Colombians were already preparing themselves psychologically for the inevitability of a first-round exit.

Something at least had been learned from USA 94.Their certainty that they would win the 1994 World Cup was a quaint reminder of Latin American *patria*, the unswerving conviction that nothing could be better, no team could be stronger than Colombia, that no result was more certain or more fitting than glorious victory for the Republic. It was also a horrific reminder of the danger of living a cycle of impossible hopes. As Colombia reeled from its undignified defeat, Ricardo Muñoz confronted Andrés Escobar in a car park outside a disco in the city of Medellín. He congratulated the 27-year-old defender on his own goal against the United States, which had sealed Colombia's sorry fate, and then fired six bullets into his chest. Helped by a ban on the sale of alcohol in the 24 hours either side of Colombia's matches, fans in 1998 learnt to be humble and soberly realistic about their team's prospects. As the opening encounter with Romania drew near, everyone from coach Hernán Darío "Bolillio" Gómez to newspaper columnists to taxi drivers was anxious not to stick their neck out and forecast great things for the team.

But as kick-off time approached, no amount of level-headedness could prevent fans at home from whipping themselves into feverish excitement. For a couple of hours before the game, the capital Bogotá was brought to a standstill by massive horn-blowing, flag-waving traffic jams before a deserted hush fell over the city, and the excitement moved indoors.

In fashionable north Bogotá, offices and shopping centres erected video screens for their employees and customers, which attracted the largest crowds. Overdressed and painted ladies, struggling under the weight of their jewellery, nervously touched up their make-up and rubbed shoulders with businessmen and bankers. Usually well-starched of clothes and character, Bogotá's elite descended, delicately, into a football crowd mentality. In the city centre, small-time emerald dealers and shopkeepers shut up their businesses and jostled for space outside TV shops with street urchins and heavily armed policemen. The prospect of 90 minutes with a semi-automatic pressed, albeit unthreateningly, in the ribs did nothing to dampen expectations and excitement in the street.

But nowhere was the atmosphere more charged than in Abysmo – a sleazy salsa bar famed for strong alcohol, rough cocaine and being the centre of Bogotá's thriving transvestite community. Firewater was off the menu, but in an atmosphere heavy with cigarette smoke and perfume the city's she-males whooped and wolf-whistled as the TV cameraman took a lingering, full-length look at each of Colombia's players.

In the end the country's radio and TV commentators could not resist a last minute burst of over-optimism. Five minutes before kick-off, they were well into their usual pre-match ritual. This consists largely of picking the other team apart until they are ready to be devoured by Colombia. The opposing team is made up of ageing veterans long past it, whippersnappers with no experience and mediocre tacticians. Of course, the trainer has done his best, and the No 9 is quite handy, but...

Imagine the shock, then, when bang on 45 minutes this motley bunch of Romanian amateurs took the lead. The commentators managed only the weakest rendition of their traditional long-drawn out "*Goool*" and then fell silent with the rest of the country. Even their relished half-time massacre of the referee was distinctly downbeat. By the end of the game Mondragón's saves were getting louder cheers than the team's stumbling efforts towards Romania's penalty area. A certain acceptance was already settling in.

The final whistle was greeted, as is often the case, by a remarkable switch in the opinions of the commentators. Colombia had put up a sterling fight, faced as they had been by a team of ruthlessly trained European football machines who were well on their way to the final. Back in Bogotá subdued and tearful crowds made their way home. Among those with their cheeks streaked in mascara was the reigning Miss Bogotá, Karen Guaqueta. "I just adore Tino," she told reporters through her tears. "It was very wrong of Darío Gómez to take him off with only five minutes to go." Beauty contests are still hugely popular in Colombia and her comments were given great play by the Gómez-hostile press the following day. They also proved to be remarkably astute.

One hapless columnist tried to put a brave face on Colombia's defeat. "Look on the bright side," he encouraged his readers. His first argument for an optimistic outlook, of course, was the heroic performance of keeper Mondragón. But otherwise, his reasons to be cheerful lacked a little conviction. Despite the defeat, he wrote, there was no trouble in Lyon. In fact there was a party with Colombian music and Colombian women, who were infinitely better than

French or Romanian ones, and, in that sense, Colombia had won.

One of Colombia's substitutes had got up at half-time and given each member of the team a pat on the back which was a nice gesture, and some of the players had tried quite hard. The rest of the press was happy to roast Darío Gómez. "Four years down the drain," wailed one paper. While Argentina's Daniel Passarella had been busy building a team ready for 2002, Gómez had done nothing, it argued. The only changes in the disastrous 1994 team were that they were now four years older, four years slower, four years more disgruntled, demotivated and apathetic.

But there was worse to come. The next day Miss Bogotá proved she either had a hotline to Faustino Asprilla or could read his mind. "I was victimised when I was substituted and there is favouritism within the squad," Tino the Octopus, as he is known for his flailing gait, told a Colombian radio reporter on a shopping trip to Paris. Asprilla and his coach have had their fair share of fall-outs, and in the interests of team unity Gómez sent the former Newcastle striker packing. Back home the press launched a second offensive, and Gómez came out fighting. "I'm leaving at the end of the tournament, and if you've got a replacement lined up, send him right now," he blustered.

With arguably their biggest star out of the team and divided loyalties within the squad, it was no surprise that Colombia were not exactly at their best against Tunisia. By now other old-timers were under attack at home. Even the saint-like figure of Carlos Valderrama came in for some gentle rebuffs. Known as *El Pibe* (the kid), Valderrama's orange afro-perm has been the symbol of Colombian football for the past 12 years. On good days his superb vision and fine touch held the team together, but his good days had always been intermittent and, more recently, few and far between.

The team's insipid 1-0 victory over Tunisia was good enough reason for a brief burst of wild celebration among Colombia's goal-starved followers at home. Some face had been saved, and there was always a possibility that they might just beat England. But the country never quite recovered from the fall-out of the Romania defeat, and there was little fighting talk in the run-up to the England game.

And if the team was respectfully wary of the encounter, Colombian fans were by all accounts terrified by "*los 'ooliganes*". My efforts to point out that not every English fan in the stadium was a mindless thug were greeted with great amusement. "Aha, now the boot's on the other foot," they laughed. "It's not nice to be branded a nation of violent brutes. And, of course, we are all drug traffickers too." They have a point.

When Mondragón shouldered away Scholes's shot in only the second minute, my adversaries in front of the telly crossed themselves frantically. There was an anguished howl when Anderton hammered in England's first after 20 minutes, and another, which seemed to echo round Bogotá, nine minutes later, when the Colombian wall flinched, allowing Beckham's curling free kick to fly past Mondragón's outstretched hand. From there on in the scene was set. Valderrama and his flaccid crew were on their way home, but Colombia's fans still found one last reason to celebrate the acrobatics of their keeper. Farid Mondragón did indeed prevent an English romp, and when the final whistle blew he collapsed in the goalmouth and wept. Back home millions shed tears with him and warmed to the sight of first Michael Owen and then David Seaman trying to comfort their new hero.

The papers the next day paid homage to the valiant Mondragón and bade a series of farewells, not only to France 98, but to a ten-year era in Colombian football, and to the team built by the ebullient Francisco Maturana. Invited to give an international lecture, Maturana once promised to show his audience a video which contained all the secrets of great football. After playing 20 minutes of a classical concert, the former national coach got up and walked off, pausing only briefly to declare: "Gentlemen, football is a feeling, and those who don't live with the same intensity of passion as you see in those musicians will never make it."

Maturana was well known for his outlandishness and, throwaway though his "seminar" might have seemed, passion is something which his more dour successor Darío Gómez has failed to instil in the same team. He has also failed to instil discipline and commitment, add his critics. Now Gómez is gone too, and on his departure was given fairly short shrift by the press. In contrast their farewell to *El Pibe* was positively gushing, with pages of praise, tributes and anecdotes.

The World Cup is always obliged to share centre stage with politics in Colombia, where presidential elections fall at the end of June. Comparison between the fate of the football team and the state of the nation are inevitable, and this time around they are particularly apt. Colombia is in a mess, with an escalating civil war and crumbling economy. The country's new president Andrés Pastrana was elected on his "back to the drawing board" reform proposals to put the country on the rails, and the press is convinced their football team needs the same treatment.

Pastrana promises to end political corruption, and here too football commentators see a parallel. Gone are the days when drug barons picked Colombian teams in return for their sizeable patronage, but many still complain that the national team's legitimate sponsors, not the coaching staff, run the show. Fans and critics alike echo Tino and Miss Bogotá's observations that old allegiances have led to favouritism in the squad, and all seem to agree that new blood on the pitch and a foreign coach is the only way to clean up and revitalise the Colombian game in preparation for 2002.

dog days

Mark McQuinn

Regarded by many

as the first Bulgarian novel, *Pod Igoto* (Under The Yoke), written in exile by Ivan Vazov, is a stirring account of life under the Ottoman Turks, who ruled the country from 1393 to 1878. The hero of the novel, Borimetchkata (the bear fighter) is a gigantic brawler who wreaks havoc on his enemies and stiffens the resolve of his compatriots in the final stages of the fight for freedom.

As France 98 approached, Bulgaria were in desperate need of similar heroics from their footballing equivalent, Hristo Stoichkov. Rather than hurl enemies bodily down mountains, which Borimetchkata often employed as a game plan, "Itso" had made his name by bundling them off the ball and doing them for pace before killing them off with his unerring left foot.

However, the fans were worried that at 32 the Lion of the Balkans was clearly in decline. Sacked by Barcelona four months before the start of the finals and at odds with the management of CSKA Sofia after his return home, Stoichkov's aggression was still there in abundance, but the searing pace and deadly finishing which had made him European Footballer of the Year in 1994 had upped sticks.

From April onwards, the two main topics of conversation in the "toto cafes" and bars were, sadly, the same as they had been at the start of the decade – the corruption that is choking the life out of Bulgaria's nascent liberal democracy, and Stoichkov. A toto cafe is one with an official football pools licence, and is generally a small, sweaty place that would provide a year's worth of work for even the most lax health and safety official. Fans spend long hours there arguing over the minutiae of European football, since the pools in Bulgaria is based on matches from a variety of countries. Detailed knowledge of form, injuries and gossip continent-wide is considered vital if that elusive jackpot is to be hit.

The morning toto shift involves consuming espressos so strong that the caffeine rush can induce manic coupon filling followed by irritable reappraisal and a plethora of messed up forms. By contrast, the afternoon shift is more likely to be a relaxed affair, helped along by a large intake of *rakia*, Bulgarian brandy, served in 100g shots. To the uninitiated, *rakia* induces a reaction similar to that of Tom on realising that yet again Jerry has tricked him into standing in the middle of the railway tracks with an express train bearing down on him at top speed. For the unwary, even a mild session inevitably leads to the belief that they could correctly forecast the entire results of the next five World Cups, never mind the laughably easy task of working out the score of Real Betis v Valencia.

In these life-affirming academies the view was that a heroic swansong from the Dog, as Stoichkov is known, was necessary if Bulgaria were to qualify for the second round. Everyone recognised that Krassy Balakov had been excellent for Stuttgart over the season, but he was also seen as a quiet lad, whose trademark is tireless and undemonstrative team play allied to great accuracy from free kicks. Stoichkov, by contrast, was still touted as the potential hero on account of his undeniable presence on and off the field, which had so often galvanised team-mates and unnerved opponents. Moreover, there was a general feeling among the fans, perhaps for the first time, that Stoichkov had overstepped the mark in his behaviour in the run-up to the finals and consequently that he owed the Bulgarian people one in France.

First, he had publicly called coach Hristo Bonev a "Mr Nobody" and refused to play in several of the qualifiers. This was particularly insulting given that Bonev, nicknamed Zuma, is one of a tiny group almost as revered by fans for their playing records as Stoichkov – he was Bulgarian Player of the Year three times and was one of the few to distinguish himself in the 1970 World Cup team. Fans from Plovdiv were particularly upset as both Stoichkov and Bonev are from the city. *Plovdivchani* take their rivalry with Sofia as seriously as any other self-respecting citizens of second cities and were therefore furious at two of their most distinguished sons squabbling in public, giving an excuse for the *Sofiantsi* to trot out their favourite line about "provincial peasants".

Stoichkov stayed away until Bulgaria's fourth qualifier, the home match against Luxembourg. On the eve of the game, June 7th, he phoned Bonev on his mobile with the gracious message: "It's Itso, your namesake, I'm coming to play in the match." Bonev immediately hung up, saying later he thought it was a hoaxer. The fans largely sided with Bonev, particularly after Stoichkov's ulterior motive was revealed in the press.

Just before the match Puma had contacted the Bulgarian Football Association and arranged a sponsorship deal, provided Bulgaria qualified. A major part of the deal was a personal £300,000 package for Stoichkov, assuming, of course, he was in the team. In general, the fans had been pleased with the spirit shown by Bonev's new-look team and Stoichkov's perceived greed did not go down well.

Stoichkov had always played up his image as a proud, independent, patriotic Bulgarian. In a country short of modern-day national heroes and with a history of domination by the Turks and

the Soviet Union, this attitude has always won him admirers. The communist regime focused strongly on the "humiliation" of Ottoman rule, which played a significant role in creating among Bulgarians an acute awareness of their suffering as a result of geopolitics. The collapse of communism in 1989 and the resulting economic, political and social chaos left Bulgarians even more desperate to find sources of national pride and self-respect. Stoichkov was one of the few such sources.

Many fine Bulgarian achievements in the arts and sciences may have gone largely unnoticed on the world stage, but at least Itso was an international figure. A considerable number of Bulgarians found his truculence and "uncultured" manner slightly embarrassing, but he struck a chord with a majority through his defiant pride in being Bulgarian. This was typified by his remark after Bulgaria's home victory over Russia that ensured qualification. Asked for his comments, Stoichkov replied: "Well, the Russians 'liberated' us twice in our history, so we were obliged to repay the debt by 'liberating' them from the World Cup." Many Bulgarians cringed, but a lot of others laughed, seeing it as the remark of a brave nationalist unafraid to bad-mouth former "oppressors" in public. The press were equally divided.

Stoichkov's financially motivated desire to return might have been more easily forgiven had he not let CSKA down in his pursuit of Mammon just a few weeks before, when he deserted them for ten days to pocket some petrodollars playing for the Saudi Arabian side Al-Nasr in the Asian Cup-Winners Cup final. For this he received $100,000 basic and a limousine for scoring the winning goal, at a time when a Gallup survey found that a quarter of Bulgarians could not afford to buy yoghurt or cheese regularly. Itso's reputation as the people's champion had been badly damaged.

After the Luxembourg match, no less a figure than the Bulgarian president, Petar Stoyanov, stepped in to negotiate the return of Stoichkov to the side. He was the ideal person since as well as being the president he is a keen sports fan, a personal friend of both the protagonists and is also from Plovdiv. Failure was not an option and Stoichkov duly returned, to the annoyance of the other old guard heroes of 1994, Trifon Ivanov, Krassy Balakov and Emil Kostadinov.

Although Bulgaria were impressive in the win over Russia that guaranteed qualification, optimism was in short supply. The traditional Bulgarian World Cup preparation formula – quarrels among the players, quarrels between the players and the management and quarrels between the players and the press – had worked remarkably well at USA 94. Four years on, however, the public were of the opinion that a new strategy should be employed based around innovations like co-operation, team spirit and forward planning.

Despite their forebodings about the team's chances, most people were determined to make a party of the finals. For many, the first stage of this plan involved buying a bigger television set, to the surprise and delight of the retailers given the parlous state of the economy. Where the money came from no one knows. Several of the proud new owners were interviewed on the national news. When asked why he had felt the need to buy a bigger television for the World Cup finals, one replied that as a patriotic Bulgarian he had throughout his life played his part in maintaining the national pastime of arguing with anyone and everyone about everything and anything. However, he had always felt that most of the time he hadn't known much about the subjects he argued about. A big, spanking new television would allow him to see the details of matches clearly, thereby allowing him to argue from a reasonable knowledge base, which would shock his friends.

Two World Cup songs dominated the airwaves all over the country. *E na sveta ne puk, nie pak sme tuk* (Although the world doesn't give a damn, we're here again) was set to the tune of *Every Breath You Take* and caused mass, drunken singing every night at every bar and cafe in the land. The words struck a chord with Bulgarians, many of whom see themselves, with considerable justification, as perennial outsiders in Europe, ignored, cheated on or generally mistreated by the rest of the continent.

The song had a close rival in the shape of a parody of a *chalga*, a traditional piece of Balkan folk music played by street performers, written by the presenters of *Ku-ku*, a satirical television show. The programme mercilessly ridicules the Bulgarian establishment and is therefore massively popular, providing jokes, songs and sketches which are repeated endlessly in cafes and bars. Their song was also played everywhere in Bulgaria and the whole nation took to chanting the surreal chorus:

> *Zuma lays down the heavy word*
> *Our system is 4-4-2*

The players also enjoyed singing it and took it to the preparation camp in France, where it was played so much that Bonev eventually banned it.

Not all of the players' antics at the preparation camp were so well received by the public back home. First, a French television crew filmed many of the players smoking after meals. Goalkeeper Bobby Mihailov earnestly explained that this was part of traditional Bulgarian culture and therefore more important than football. Then Lubo Penev gave an interview to *Planet Football*, a national television programme. Penev ignored the first question from the journalist and instead launched an attack on his old-fashioned microphone, shouting: "Are you kidding me? What kind of mike is this? Do you want me to give you money to buy a new one? Don't mess me about." The programme makers ran Penev's outburst without comment as part of the interview, sending his already low stock with the fans to subterranean levels.

After the excitement of the pre-tournament shenanigans, the first match was inevitably going to be a disappointment. However, no one believed it could be as dull as the scoreless draw with Paraguay turned out to be. The biggest talking point was the referee's failure to award a penalty when Stoichkov was checked in the area early on. Most saw it as an outrage, but a few pointed out that Stoichkov had conned so many decisions out of referees over the years that there could be few complaints about one going the other way.

The uneventful nature of the match did not stop one of Plovdiv's *bortsi* (literally "wrestlers", who dominate large scale criminal activities) commemorating it in style. He sat on the balcony of his tenth floor apartment firing off round after round from his Kalashnikov and swigging from a bottle of Johnnie Walker. In the small hours the neighbours called the police, who, almost certainly with great reluctance, paid him a visit.

When asked why he had been firing his gun for so long he replied that he was celebrating after the match. When the officers politely pointed out that there was little to celebrate, he informed them that he was firing his gun to commiserate. On being told that there wasn't that much to be upset about either, the wrestler started to lose patience, stating forcefully that he would be out of the country for the next two matches and therefore wanted to celebrate and commiserate in advance as he was not sure how the results would go. This was good enough for the police, who did, however, pluck up the courage to ask him when he might finish. The wrestler seemed astonished at such an obtuse question and tersely informed them that he would stop when the bullets ran out – of course.

The *bortsi* are a frightening phenomenon of post-communist Bulgaria. They are products of isolated sports schools, where they spend their formative years undergoing ferocious training in wrestling and other combat sports. Life in the schools is organised around absolute obedience to the patriarch – the trainer – and produces a value system based around the worship of physical strength, violence and group loyalty. Since the fall of communism they have openly engaged in drug trafficking, prostitution rackets, car stealing and extortion, usually under the patronage of ex-officers from the Bulgarian secret police.

Dressed in Armani suits, dripping in gold and never far away from their brand new four-wheel-drive jeeps or Ferraris, the "no-necks" dominate the most expensive cafes, bars and restaurants. Their swaggering contempt for the rest of society has done much to create a climate of fear and resentment in the country. A friend was watching the Paraguay match in a hotel bar when a group of *bortsi* came in. When Stoichkov was brought down, he grabbed the arm of a wrestler without thinking, shouting "penalty". On realising with horror what he had done, he apologised profusely. The wrestler good-naturedly brushed it aside, saying: "No problem, it's the closest a loser like you is ever going to get to an Armani suit, so I hope you enjoyed it."

The fans felt Bulgaria were unlucky against Nigeria. The only gripe was about the finishing of the senior players, as Kostadinov and Stoichkov squandered chances they would have buried two years previously. This rekindled the argument about whether the team should have stuck with the younger players that Bonev selected before the old guard muscled their way back in. Being part of that younger group was no laughing matter if one believes the rumours filtering back to Bulgaria that Stoichkov had slapped several of them during half-time in the Nigeria match. In fact these stories were largely discounted by the fans, who were convinced that he had punched them, as Itso was too manly to resort to slapping.

So it was all or nothing against Spain, and the snug bar philosophers were going for a resounding "nothing". But there was still plenty to distract attention from the impending disaster. First Stoichkov decided that he should inform the public about Spanish history and politics. To this end he gave an interview in which he explained that Catalonia is not Spain and should in fact be independent. Furthermore, Itso solemnly anounced that in support of this goal he would be wearing a T-shirt with "Independence for Catalonia" printed on it, which he would expose when he scored. Surprisingly, most people thought he would do better to concentrate on preparing for the match rather than sounding off about another country's internal affairs. Some even went so far as to mention that it was not 100 per cent certain that he would score.

Obviously tired and emotional from his exertions in explaining the complexities of Spanish history and politics to the folks back home, Stoichkov, along with Penev, then missed training and "disappeared". The most popular rumour was that they had used their extensive Spanish connections to negotiate a bribe to throw the match. A great deal of evidence was put forward to support this theory. First, both Stoichkov and Penev have extensive playing experience in Spain. Second, both speak fluent Spanish. Third, well, there were two pieces of pretty damaging evidence against them. The two surfaced in the camp the next day claiming implausibly they had been there all along and had merely been sleeping heavily.

Whatever the truth of the matter, the pressure was starting to tell on Bonev. He collapsed unconscious before a training session and looked a shadow of the confident figure who had guided Bulgaria through the qualifiers. The match itself plunged the country into disbelief. That Bulgarians are a passionate people was evidenced by the number of television sets hurled out of windows at the end. This is something of a recent tradition, but it's a grand gesture when you take into account the amount of work that most Bulgarians have to put in to afford one.

Strangely, many of the "television heroes" cited the post-match statements of the commentators as the final straw. These were leaden castigations of the whole campaign read out in such a stulti-fying manner that it was obvious they had been prepared in advance. New rumours quickly spread. Bonev had been bribed by clubs to include certain of their players so that they would be in the shop window. Stoichkov had threatened and terrified the younger players at half-time, so they could not concentrate in the second half. Different factions among the players had refused to pass to each other. A few even put forward the outlandish theory that the team was simply not very good. This was quickly discounted as being ludicrously fanciful.

That the campaign would end in Bonev's resignation was inevitable. What was not foreseen was the name of the new coach to spearhead Bulgaria's Euro 2000 efforts. The press and the fans had narrowed it down to a shortlist of three – the former coach Dimitar Penev, Georgi Vassilev, the only Bulgarian coach to have guided three different teams to the championship, and Petar Zehtinski, the coach of the national junior team. Yet when the announcement came, the new man turned out to be... Hristo Bonev. Immediately the media thronged the offices of the football association trying to get an explanation. The sight of the BFA officials going through a Keystone Cops routine, running away from the press, dodging down side streets, and trying to brush journalists aside, bluster their way through and pretend they hadn't heard questions was one of the most popular programmes on Bulgarian television for years.

Bonev himself was the star of the show. He pretended to have such a bad sore throat that he could not speak and promptly disappeared to Turkey for two weeks for a "rest cure". He returned to announce that of the old guard only Stoichkov and Penev, his chief tormentors, would be included in the national squad for forthcoming games.

Thus, Bulgaria's chaotic World Cup 1998 campaign closed as it had begun, with the fans not knowing whether to laugh or cry. Nothing could be surer proof of the lure of the game than the fact that Bonev, a man revered in the country for his playing career, a decent and honest person and reasonably secure financially, would again want to put himself through the particular hell of trying to guide Bulgaria through a major international football tournament.

Thanks to Nikolai Nedelchev and Pressiana Georgieva

onward virgin soldiers

Mike Mitchell

Mexico went to the World Cup

looking, to their supporters, like the chronicle of a quick return foretold, but instead ended up with a heroes' welcome after their first qualification for the second round in finals held in Europe. Patriotic fervour first turned sour in November 1997, when 110,000 fans at the Azteca stadium saw the home side draw 0-0 with a ten-man United States side in what should have been a routine CONCACAF qualifier. The fans got what they wanted as their derisive jeers were answered with the departure of coach Bora Milutinovic.

His replacement, Manuel Lapuente, at first fared little better, even though Mexico finished top of the CONCACAF group. The fans were less than impressed with draws against Costa Rica and Jamaica, to be followed by weeks of embarrassing performances against European league sides. In the run-up to the finals the film *Titanic* was doing the rounds of Mexican cinemas, offering an obvious nickname for a team which many feared would founder even when confronted by South Korea, let alone the looming European icebergs of Holland and Belgium.

But the newspapers were left clutching at new metaphors when Luis "Matador" Hernandez suddenly refound his killer instinct against Korea. Previously Hernandez's biggest contribution to the World Cup campaign had been the billboards plastered all over the country with his reclining figure and dyed blonde locks advertising underwear.

If Hernandez's two goals got the crowds roaring in front of the big screens in downtown Mexico City's baking colonial-era streets, the Korea match was also memorable for the unveiling by Cuauhtemoc Blanco – named after the last Aztec emperor who refused to surrender and was tortured to death by Spanish conquistadors – of what English-speakers now call the "Blanco bounce". As it turned out, Blanco's trick of grabbing the ball between his ankles and hopping over opponents' feet proved about as effective when it mattered as the flamboyant displays of defiance by his famous namesake.

Nevertheless, Mexico's bright start whipped the country into full-blown World Cup fever. Bars advertised special two-for-one offers to entice customers, although the time difference with France meant not a few arrived late for work and unsteady on their feet after liquid breakfasts. However, they did so in the almost certain knowledge that no one would mind, or even notice. Dealing on the battered local stock market slowed to a standstill as brokers took a break from dumping shares to watch the national side, the normally smog-laden air cleared as motorists forsook the 18-million strong capital's streets for safer havens by TV screens, and building-site workers downed pneumatic drills and piledrivers to hear the radio commentary.

However, not everyone in Mexico was enjoying the tournament. The night before the Korea game saw United Nations High Commissioner for Human Rights Mary Robinson express concern over the "alarming situation" in poverty-stricken Chiapas, a state with a largely indigenous population at the southern tip of Mexico, near the border with Guatemala. Robinson spoke two days after a bloody clash between the army and alleged supporters of Zapatista rebels, who rose up against the government at the beginning of 1994.

Eight Indians said to be Zaptista supporters and a policeman died in the clash at the village of El Bosque, adding a new atrocity to a conflict that has killed hundreds over the past four years. The government said an army column was ambushed, but human rights groups noticed grisly press photos of corpses in army trucks and suspected a massacre. Several press columnists were of the view that the government deliberately upped the ante in Chiapas while the public's attention was diverted by the World Cup. Another clash earlier the same week between security forces and alleged guerrillas killed 11 in Guerrero, another poor southern state where many, as in Chiapas, often do not have electricity, let alone televisions for watching football matches.

Whatever the government's intentions, the team were certainly doing their best to keep Mexico's mind off such uncomfortable reminders of reality for as long as possible. Their 2-2 draw with Belgium, after being two goals down, was widely seen as a moral victory, but still left the prospects of reaching the second round about as certain as clean elections back home – something you can occasionally glimpse in the distance, but never really believe will be achieved.

Parish priests around this traditionally devoutly Catholic country began to call on divine help before the final group game against Holland, by dressing wooden figures of baby Jesus in Mexico's green, white and red strip. Many statues of Mexico's most revered religious icon, the Virgin of Guadalupe, wore a No 12 shirt to indicate her symbolic presence on the bench for the national squad. The Guadalupe fixation is significant not simply as a religious symbol, but is also closely identified with Mexico itself – banners of the home-grown cult led Mexico's fighters for independence from

Spain in the early 19th century. She is therefore the natural first port of call for prayers to assist the national team.

Jose Guadalupe Hernandez, parish priest at the rural church of Our Lady of Lightning in central Puebla state said he led prayers to Guadalupe while 100 of his flock crowded in front of a big screen he had installed in the nave of his church.

"We asked the son [Jesus] of player No 12 to give the strength of a buffalo to our side so they should neither get tired nor injured, and an Apache's dead eye to score many goals," Hernandez said. "We are sure our Virgin will grant our boys calm, serenity and wisdom, and the spark needed for timely play. May the game be crowned with the culmination of a classic goal."

Those prayers seemed to be answered when Luis Hernandez scored his last-minute equaliser against the sceptical, rationalistic Dutch, and Mexico went collectively beserk. President Ernesto Zedillo was granted an almost instant post-match interview with manager Lapuente and his "matador", courtesy of the pro-government Televisa network, which has a monopoly on broadcasting Mexico's international games. Zedillo, in a phrase more than slightly tinged with machismo, proclaimed that Mexico's team had shown they "had the size" to deal with the competition and that, once more, they had shown the conquering spirit with which Mexico could overcome its problems.

Critics were quick to point out that the Zedillo administration had not been conspicuously successful in showing the same conquering spirit, wallowing as it was in controversy over a $65 billion bank bailout and repeated budget cuts due to dwindling income from oil exports. Political columnists wondered aloud whether Zedillo was trying to wrap himself in the national team's colours in a bid to bask in a brief glimpse of glory and recover some kudos for his Institutional Revolutionary Party, which is struggling to retain the office it has held since 1929 in the face of economic crisis and corruption scandals.

On the very day of the Holland match, a jailed former chief of police admitted he had taken hundreds of thousands of dollars in bribes from drug gangs for protection. On that same day, police arrested the family of Daniel Arizmendi, head of a kidnapping ring which gained notoriety for slicing the ears off its victims and sending them to relatives to speed up ransom payments.

But who was going to stay at home worrying about the budget deficit or trivial cases of mutilation when there was a World Cup triumph to celebrate? Thousands poured into city squares in a mad party as the war cry "Yes, we can!" started by a TV station became "Yes, we could!" But the festivities soured in Mexico's central avenue, Paseo de la Reforma, when crowds battled with riot police blocking the way to the nation's Angel of Independence monument, the traditional site for celebrating national victories. Three press photographers at the scene had to be rushed to hospital suffering from head wounds after they were trapped under a barrage of missiles thrown by rioters.

The prayers of the faithful proved ineffective in the second round, as Mexico tempted fate by taking the lead and ceded the role of comeback kings to the ever-willing Germans. Still, Luis Hernandez came back to Mexico with four goals from as many games and a feeling that he might yet make a more successful excursion from Mexico than his recent inglorious time at Argentina's Boca Juniors.

With a little more nerve, Mexico might have claimed the prize that fell to Croatia of humiliating the Germans. On the other hand, they earned the thanks of a grateful football world by eliminating the dreadfully negative Belgians. And for the vast majority of Mexican fans that was enough. Their team went down fighting and honour was restored. Or, as Manuel Lapuente put it: "We leave with our faces to the sun."

midsummer night's dream

Knut Are Tvedt

Prior to the World Cup,

Norway had gone 14 matches without defeat. Having prospered against Brazil, France (away) and Denmark (away), the feeling became alarmingly widespread that Norway were capable of winning the World Cup. The coach Egil "Drillo" Olsen did nothing to dampen optimism. We could go all the way, he agreed, though he took care to add that he did not think it was likely.

But after all, so the thinking went, who could stop us? The first game would be against Morocco. They had some good technical players, but were not very well organised. Norway's main strength is organisation and discipline. So, no problem. The second, crucial, game would be against Scotland. Nobody could see how Norway could reach the knockout stage without beating Scotland. The Scots were without any really skilful players, and the general consensus was that they were not organised at all. The only thing to be afraid of was their fighting spirit.

The third game would be Brazil. Difficult, but who had beaten Brazil last year? Besides, according to Olsen, the Brazilians were "a little overpraised". And anyway, if we could beat Morocco and Scotland, we wouldn't have to get anything from Brazil. That would take us to the last 16. The next game would probably be against Italy, or maybe Chile. Italy had beaten us at USA 94, but now they had an ageing team. A good performance in the second round would take us to the quarter-finals and possibly a meeting with one of the other outsiders, like South Africa – or Denmark.

The average Norwegian would be content with reaching the quarter-finals. Most outsiders would. The first inkling that this might prove an elusive goal was the realisation that everybody else also thought they could reach the last eight. The Norwegian public was very surprised to hear that both the Moroccans and the Scots felt quite confident about getting through from Group A.

World Cup fever took hold in earnest the day before the match against Morocco, as *VG*, the largest newspaper in Norway, devoted eight pages to the national team. The other leading tabloid newspaper, *Dagbladet*, hired a helicopter to bring some out-of-focus pictures of Norway's "secret" training camp. In Oslo, you could detect a certain tension as people prepared for the match. At home we always adjust our eating and drinking to the games we watch. That night we had a typical Norwegian dinner; fried mackerel with sour cream and boiled potatoes, along with Norwegian beer and aquavit.

The team's performance, however, was not quite as typical, nor as satisfying, with the defence clearly unnerved by the speed of the Moroccans. There were no excuses afterwards: we were lucky to get a draw. Morocco played well and we were very nervous, especially in defence where Dan Eggen in particular was singled out for his blunders. The next day the newspapers tried to play down expectations. Maybe they could play a bit in other parts of the world, too. But there would be plenty of time to recover before the Scotland match.

Norway's mediocre showing was hardly ameliorated by Olsen,

who left the press conference after the game without answering a question. Olsen, who has eyesight problems, was upset by a bright TV light being shone in his face and walked out when his request to turn it off was ignored. The collective sulk was completed by Kjetil Rekdal, never one to indulge in self-mockery, who was upset by people poking fun at his yellow boots, particularly since they highlighted a performance that was less than outstanding. "People attacking me for being lazy and wearing yellow boots, it's just too ridiculous," he said. Asked if it annoyed him that people said he was running slowly, he replied: "Yes, because I don't. We have tests to prove that. But my style of running is deceptive."

The next day the Norwegian players were given a night off, and Henning Berg and Erik Mykland went to a night club until 5am. At last, the Norwegian tabloid press had something to write about. *VG* gave over 13 pages to the story, including interviews with the bartenders and other guests. No one could remember if the two players had drunk alcohol during their visit, even though the club was packed with journalists. As one reporter from *Bergens Tidende* put it later: "It was difficult enough to take care of ourselves, never mind watching what others were drinking." Olsen told the press that the two had not had a drink, which meant that they did not have to be sent home. The general reaction back home, however, was to wonder what you would do in a nightclub until five in the morning if you weren't drinking.

The coverage of this story, combined with his bit part in the team's matches, led to Mykland's premature retirement from international football. He was replaced by Ståle Solbakken for the match with Scotland, although Olsen insisted it had nothing to do with the night club affair. When Mykland was asked about this, however, he answered: "Nice weather today, isn't it?"

Everyone in Norway expected a comfortable victory. On the front page of *VG* there was a picture of a "typical" Scottish football fan, stripped to the waist in a tartan cap and kilt with nothing underneath. **Play The Kilt Off Them!** said the headline. But they didn't.

Instead, it was another lucky draw. For the second time our usual strengths became weaknesses: we were badly organised and ill-disciplined. We took the lead this time, and yet still lost the initiative in the second half. Still, Brazil beat Morocco, so the chances of qualifying were reasonable.

Norway's downcast mood at the mediocrity of the team's performances was scarcely improved by the eagerness of the Swedes to revel in our lack of success. Norwegian fans are always very keen to read Swedish newspapers and watch Swedish TV to know how our neighbours, for so long the top dogs in Scandinavian football, are reacting to Norway's performances – all the more so this time around when their own team had not even qualified. It did not make congenial reading. The Swedish newspaper *Aftonbladet*, which had described Norway as the dullest and poorest side in the World Cup earlier in the tournament, now went into overdrive, damning the Norwegian performance against Scotland as "a disgrace to Nordic football".

June 23rd, the day of the match with Brazil, is celebrated as midsummer's eve in Norway. It coincides with the end of the school term and the start of the summer holidays. People go out in boats, sit around open fires, eat prawns and dance. And it doesn't get dark – even in the south, we have daylight throughout the night. This year was different. All the advertisements for any kind of entertainment that was going on emphasised that the evening's events would be over by nine, or that you could watch TV on the premises. I was on the south coast, where the boats usually go out to the skerries on midsummer's night. But not this year. Everyone stayed in to watch the game.

It was worth it to see one of the most exciting matches in Norwegian football history. When Norway scored their winner from the penalty spot two minutes from time, everybody ran outdoors to celebrate. In Oslo and other cities there was all-night dancing in the street. No sports event has ever been the cause for so much celebration in Norway, apart from the 1994 Winter Olympics at

Lillehammer. But this was different; impulsive and unbelievable. We'd beaten Brazil. In the World Cup. All the major newspapers plastered the victory over their front pages with headlines like **Thank You** and **The Miracle**. Sweden's *Aftonbladet* shamelessly proclaimed **Today We Are All Norwegians!**, devoting six pages to the match and the "revenge of the prophet" (Olsen).

Sweden's place on the Scandinavian bandwagon was at least earned by the part their television cameras played in demonstrating that Tore André Flo had indeed had his shirt pulled by Junior Baiano in the incident that led to Norway's penalty. Prior to that even some Norwegian newspapers had questioned its validity. However, it was not enough to convince the Moroccans, who asserted that the pictures showed a completely different incident from earlier in the match, and that it was outside the penalty area anyway.

Expectations before the second-round match against Italy were both high and low. No one doubted that Norway were capable of winning. In fact, one could argue plausibly that the Norwegian side was better than the Italians. On the other hand, this was the World Cup. Italy seldom frighten anyone in friendly matches. But in the World Cup finals, they had only lost one crucial game since 1978 (against France in 1986). In 1982 they became world champions. In 1990 they went out on penalties in the semi-final. In 1994 they lost on penalties in the final.

And there was one more thing. For Norway, the official target had already been reached by making it through to the last 16. Somewhere we had to stop. For Italy, the World Cup started here. Their aim was to go to the semi-finals at least. They could cause us more trouble than we could cope with. And so they did. Vieri scored an early goal, and that was enough. The Italians never play better than they have to. And that afternoon they did not have to play very well. Norway seemed tired, perhaps happy just to have got past the group stage, and Pagliuca in the Italian goal had a comfortable afternoon, easily snapping up all the high punts from the Norwegian midfielders.

A few critics tried to make the point that Norway had become a bit too predictable, with their long, high passes battering impotently at a well-organised defence. Olsen would have none of it. "We were not cynical enough," he maintained. "We should have spent more time on defensive organisation, as we had new players coming in." Small wonder, then, that the rest of the world was glad to get rid of us. But the Norwegians? We loved it throughout.

Apart from our affection for Olsen, which may have seemed perverse to outsiders, there were more obvious causes for satisfaction. The press were happy to report that there had been no trouble involving our supporters. After the defeat by Italy some bars in Marseille had been drunk dry by Norwegians, but there were no reports of fighting. A few days after the match against Scotland, the Bordeaux city council inserted a full-page advertisement in one of the leading Norwegian newspapers, where they thanked the Norwegian fans for their behaviour. "We miss you already," they said, "and we will welcome all Norwegians back to Bordeaux."

Having beaten Brazil and exited at the same stage as England, few were in the mood to complain about the team's performance. Indeed, it was England's defeat against Argentina that produced one of the most memorable moments of Norway's World Cup, thanks to Arne Scheie, the Norwegian equivalent of John Motson. Scheie is an ardent England fan, who travelled round the country in during the 1966 World Cup, living in a tent. Always the man for an unexpected fact, Scheie seized his moment as David Beckham was sent off. "Isn't it odd," he remarked, "how every sending-off for England has occurred in the month of June?" And he went on to name each player and the game concerned.

So we went out, by and large content. There was one small scandal, which went largely unreported.The Norwegian FA promised that 980 tickets for the Italy match in Marseille were to be sold to Norwegian fans outside the Stade Vélodrome the day before the game. People queued nearly the whole day, but when the sales started, a spokesman from the FA admitted that 230 tickets had "disappeared" from the quota. The announcement caused an uproar among the waiting fans, but thankfully tickets were easy to come by outside the ground on the day of the game, with black market prices well below face value. It emerged later that the FA had short-changed the fans by selling the 230 tickets to a travel agency, whose packages for the Italy game alone cost around £1,000.

All such minor events were forgotten, however, in the rush to mark Olsen's last match in charge after eight years as Norway's coach. "If we do not win the World Cup, my last game will be a defeat," he had said before the tournament. Yet few complained about such an exit. The Norwegian media spent more time paying tribute to Olsen than mourning over the defeat. The biggest newspapers had **Thank You, Drillo** on their front pages. A song with the same title had been recorded by three of the players before the tournament and the video was played over and over again on national TV. There was not a dry eye in the nation. Then we settled down to support Denmark.

Thanks to Ole P. Pedersen

paying the penalty

Ivan Briscoe

The man behind

was about to have a nervous seizure, and his spittle was getting in my ear. He had started quietly, confidently, with just a firm "England doesn't exist" to put his mind at rest, but extra time was turning him reddish. Now he was bellowing it out, working up a froth: "England does not exist. Seaman does not exist."

Not much else existed from kick-off either. Most of the England midfield, at one stage or other, had not existed. Nor the referee, who definitely did not exist, and whose decisions were also liable to non-being. While people around him were more convinced that the English existed, and were putting the boot in on their mothers, he just shook violently and nestled on my shoulder.

"Batty doesn't exist," he said, menacingly. And in the end, he was right. It lasted only a flicker, a startled little pause before the hoarse ranks in the bar grasped that Batty's punt had been halted in mid-flight by Carlos Roa. Then the world erupted. The screen disappeared behind a hundred punching arms, and a deafening noise broke out. The man behind took a deep breath and shook my hand. His eyes shone with ecstatic sympathy. England existed after all. And it had lost.

There were maybe 30 English people in the bar, one of the few Irish pubs in Buenos Aires. But that made no difference on a match-day of such epic proportions. It was packed – as every one of the city's watering spots was – with patriotic fervour of a kind known only every four years, a here-today-and-gone-tomorrow love for all that is Argentinian.

A few of us sunken English souls escaped into the open air, but that only made matters worse. Crackers rained down from balconies, along with paper, toilet rolls, bills. I went to get a bus home, but a block away, between the lingerie stores and the cinemas, it looked like the Paris Commune had come back to life in sky blue and white and was moving in. Somehow a bus had managed to part the popular surge, and I got on. It was like watching a really bad feelgood movie after your house has burned down. The bus swerved slowly between clumps of elated pedestrians, chanting the same dirge: "If you don't jump, you're English."

The whole of Buenos Aires shone with the lustre of a massive urban makeover. I felt like a spy as I grieved through it. The drabness had gone, the pained, hassled expressions vanished, the vague sense of loss repaired. It was now lined by bright lights, stuffed with scraps of white paper, deafened by the violent tooting of car horns, and full of beautiful, dark-haired, smiling, successful people.

But the feeling that you were in Milan could only last for a while. In the centre of town, around a large, white phallus called the Obelisk, the elation had its epicentre, where thousands freely cursed the English. Teenage girls screamed their love for the "little donkey" Ariel Ortega, men beat their chests in honour of the motherland. The Obelisk, as one paper said, was "a finger saying 'fuck you' to the world". Two hours later, however, all hell broke loose. Police went in with tear gas, fans with stones, shop windows were ritually smashed, and central Buenos Aires experienced its own private *intifada*.

That is the strange thing about a World Cup in Argentina. It is never, and never can be, just a matter of football. The emotion is too intoxicating, too unreliable, it spurts out in ways it should not, it changes too many things. You have four years of bad news, crap politicians and fraudulent millionaires, they say, and then you get 30 hallucinogenic days (if you are lucky) of being a glorious, talented breed apart.

A feeling like that can have a wild and unruly sway. It can also shift a lot of merchandise. "We are sending out 22 of our best men who carry under their skin 33 million people thirsty for another cup... We need happiness of the sort that football knows how to give us," says a manic voice over film of a wet bloke swinging a huge flag, intercut with a few clips of Argentinian lakes and hills. In an advertisement for beer.

Yet, until England, the 1998 version of national chest-beating had not looked as though it was up to scratch. True, football dominated space and time – the main evening television news programmes moved their production units to France and replaced virtually all local news with detailed reports on French underwear prices and stately homes – but the vibe was different. Daniel Passarella was mean, mechanical. And the little bloke was missing, the godhead had forsaken the team and was releasing his testosterone in some shady corners of Buenos Aires. The team was just not Argentina without him.

In the first post-Maradona World Cup the country had to find its football bearings all over again. Passarella's chosen men – fast, European-based and prone to inane comments – were not the sort to inspire fervour. Beating Japan by a goal was not enough. Radio pundits clamoured for the great traditions, for "the imposition of our football on the pitch". Teams like Japan had to be pulverised by graceful dribbles from the half-way line, not just eased aside by one bit of finishing.

Inevitably, Maradona was raised in almost every discussion, as if the mere sound of his name would soothe the anxiety of living without him. Even his stick-insect striking partner Claudio Caniggia would have been an improvement, but Cani was out of favour and had been discovered swapping price-tags on shoes in a Miami shop a week before the World Cup began.

Decimating Jamaica cheered things up a bit, although even five goals failed to satisfy. "With Jamaica," wrote veteran football reporter Hector Hugo Cardozo in Argentina's biggest paper *Clarín*, "a totally precarious team without any identity, you have to vigorously impose the difference. Make them know who is who." Even during the match, several commentators seemed more interested in assessing the chances of a long line of Argentinian men who approached three conspicuously busty Jamaican fans than the fact that Batigol was registering in triplicate.

Yet despite the cavils, something was starting to happen. Argentina was walking tall again, trampling again on minor nations. To the pundits, Brazil were beatable, the Germans looked old, the Italians morose, and the French were just having a little party before getting a great big thumping. Against Croatia, on the other hand, Argentina thrust out its chest and demanded respect. Or so they said. And the streets of Buenos Aires began to put on their World Cup clothes: schools shut down, taxis sported their flags, glimpses of blue and white appeared on scarves, socks, shirts. People let the illusion run.

All neutral parties I knew thought the Croatia game insipid and slow, an irrelevant match that it would have been better to lose given England's fall earlier in the week. But a man named Marcelo Gallardo had sparked some synapse in the national psyche: with Gallardo and Ortega crisscrossing the midfield, it appeared that Argentina was rising from Diego's ashes, playing *toqueteo* (one-touch) football, not letting the Europeans get a decent sniff of the ball. It was the glorious shanty style. Even César Luis Menotti, the architect of the 1978 team and a manager known for philosophising, let rip: "Argentina wiped Croatia off the field without a problem."

As the match drew to an undramatic close, with one end of the stadium forming the sort of shirt-waving mass which shakes entire concrete stands on match days in Buenos Aires, one pundit went into high-pitched exultation: "We're the only team not to have let a goal in, we've won all our matches, we have the Cup's highest scorer – what more do you want?" The answer was simple: the scalp of the English.

That night it was all anyone could talk about. Argentinians played it confident, cocksure. "If it's a normal game, we'll win," Alejandro Prosdocimi from the sports newspaper *Olé* told me without a pause for doubt. But some admitted private fears of the abnormal, of Alan Shearer's head, of balls hurled into the penalty area as in the last few agonising minutes of the 1986 version. "That's our weakness, we don't like it in the area, we don't like the chaos," a friend conceded unwillingly.

But deep down, Argentinians had started to lock into the fount of football memory. People discussed and rediscussed Maradona's goals in the Azteca stadium, taking you through the names of each player he stripped on the way to goal. That Saturday night – just three days before the game – I ended up brandishing every fact at my disposal to convince one Argentinian devotee that England could snatch it. His answer was blunt: "We can't lose to the English. We're not allowed to lose to them."

Normally it would be hard to find a pedestrian on the shaky pavements of Buenos Aires who would declare their love of all things Argentinian. Independence Day is a chance to stay in bed, while the only people who show real interest in anything to do with the flag are primary school children, the president and the Argentinian military, two of which are widely regarded as the devil's spawn.

People descended from Italian and Spanish immigrants still quiz themselves on what exactly they are doing thousands of miles from Europe, in a vast land containing more cows than people. Football

causes such questions to be put on hold for a while. "Nationalism is the neighbour whom I smile at for the first time in years when she takes out the rubbish," mused one writer reflecting on the effect of the World Cup in a local magazine for the intelligentsia.

Suddenly, a unity of emotion grips the country. The rich talk to the poor in Buenos Aires, however fleetingly, and the indigenous Indians living off armadillo and rice in the north worry about little else but whether the village television will show the matches. The national team reflects the spread of the country: Juan Verón is a flash city type, while Carlos Roa reads the Bible and Ariel Ortega hails from the tropical regions, where at the age of one he was laid on a bed of warm cow's intestines to cure a bout of flu.

The fact that England were the opponents only served to open the valves a few turns more. Here was the common enemy, out to get whipped once again. Argentinians might adore Mick Jagger and hanker after cream tea in the Ritz, but when it comes to the English as a whole, the dominant emotion is pretty bilious. "They say that the identity of people is built when it recognises the other," wrote zeitgeist analyst Mario Wainfield on the day of the match. "They are our favourite enemy, the one we chose to define ourselves against, winning, losing, or suffering injustices." In other words: Argentina is built on not-England.

As the days dripped by before the match, the imminence of the battle in St Etienne sucked every other event out of existence. Yet more television programmes moved to France, with presenters praying aloud for victory and damning the "pirates" from Albion. Intrepid journalists nervously approached English *hooliganos* to ask how much beer they had drunk in the last 24 hours, while several brutal murders in the outskirts of Buenos Aires passed unnoticed. Relations with Argentinian friends grew noticeably strained by the prospect of combat. Their jokes about long balls and English defenders' ball control started to wear thin. Raising the spectre of Michael Owen in return caused jaws to clench.

Pundits tried to dampen the fires, hysterically repeating the "it's only a football match" line, trying to mark some moral gap between the match and the most inglorious symbol of English malevolence, the Falklands War. But by the day of the game, few people were under any illusions. It might be purely symbolic, but hell, what symbol could be better? What other symbolic event does Argentina win?

The mood in the Irish bar was feisty well before the match began. A timid English chant was met with a roaring avalanche of Argentinian stadium insults. A doctor appeared on television to give advice on what to do if struck by a heart attack. In the first half, panic switched from side to side, nation to nation, screams for another Batigol metamorphosed into keening every time Owen – described in one paper the next day simply as "that damned kid" – picked up the ball and sped away.

Somehow Javier Zanetti pulled out the "laboratory strike" to equalise in injury time, and the interval was lived on both sides like a stay of execution. People breathed deeply, reassessed the terror of that miss by Scholes, called for the entry of Gallardo and Passarella's obstinate head. English fans stood, unable to speak. After half-time, Argentina, one man up, had the ball but couldn't score. Shouting levels doubled, tripled. "That is England's 8,629th corner," bemoaned the commentator, heartily sick of it all.

Penalties were a kind of dreamland after the ebb and flow of the real thing. It was now just a question of winning, of advancing. Argentina was desperate, and poor Batty had decided not to exist.

Across the country they surged out: 30,000 in one provincial town, many more in Buenos Aires, 5,000 into a freezing cold night in Tierra del Fuego. Nurses in the main Buenos Aires psychiatric hospital were forced into emergency procedure after patients dashed themselves against beds and each other. Beneath the Obelisk, before everything got unruly, one Ricardo Palandino madly pounded his drum, the same drum his father had bought in 1982 hoping it would be of use when victory in the Malvinas was assured.

By the next day the country had settled down for a good, hard gloat.

It Was A Pleasure screamed *Clarín*, while *Olé* ran a simple **Sorry** on its cover. One reporter interpreted it as proof of a classic national trait: "That's it. We're winners." Tucked inside the sports pages, analysts berated the team for its flaws and for the way the defence had imploded at Owen's feet, but the doubts were lost in a thicket of self-love and chortling news readers. Predictably, the "it's only football" pretence passed away in the night. "Let's finish with the hypocrisy," wrote the journalist Osvaldo Pepe in a commentary in *Clarín*. "What happened yesterday in St Etienne was not a simple football match... What was on the pitch was the collective Argentinian memory, that long series of episodes – some sporting, some political – internalised since childhood, which built the image of the unpleasant Englishman, first an invader, a usurper of our riches, then a model of the dominant classes."

One English friend, drunk at the time, ended up in a heated argument with a florist who had mocked his roots, and ended up stealing 12 pink roses. Another, also drunk, tried to join in the party with a rabid scream for Argentina and got a horrible beating. I tried to swallow the defeat, but the contagion all around me made it stick in my throat. Some people were sympathetic, tuned to the bitterness a loss on penalties can produce. But it made little difference when the bus journey through the streets was still vivid in the memory. "Look, look, take a photo, they're going back to England, with a broken arse." It wasn't a song to make you feel at home.

In many ways it was the **Gotcha** style of nationalism, a mirror image of British tabloid fever carried across the Atlantic. The two xenophobias seemed to nourish each other in their extremes and feed off the insecurities of their publics. And as in England, a minority were in active rebellion: the same World Cup memories which delight in Maradona's dribbling also incorporate the deeds of 1978, when football fever managed briefly to cloak the deeds of brutal military dictatorship.

Argentinians feel guilt about their football love more than any other people. Taxi drivers will confess that they do not want

Argentina to win, arguing that victory is just more deceit. One prominent football chat show on television even veered off into an hour's debate on the nature of World Cup success shortly after the victory over Japan. "A World Cup changes nothing," the presenter spat out, "we won in 1986, we came second in 1990, and we have a terrible level of unemployment and poverty – nothing has got better." At his side, the manager in those two cups, Carlos Bilardo, mounted a defence of his work but seemed lost when asked how he could justify the mind-numbing pleasure his team had unleashed.

An academic I knew who had stridently refused to watch any match ended up during one game flinging curses at a woman on the street who had asked him why he was not screaming by the box. But as the Holland game approached, the sceptics were sidelined. Once again, the media found itself replaying the images of history, above all the final of 1978 and the euphoric face of then dictator Jorge Videla, who watched as his regime tapped the wild national passions to give itself a bit more leeway for murder. But that was not the concern now. On the day, Argentina had beaten Holland 3-1: it was a good omen.

It rained all day in Buenos Aires, a fine, constant drizzle which forced everyone to walk with their heads bowed while the grime glistened on the city's concrete. Over 1,000 policemen had occupied every part of the city centre to ward off trouble, but they were troops for a war which never happened. The bars and cafes were full but silent. One minute from the end of normal time, after a long period of total Dutch domination, Bergkamp received a long pass, trapped it and fired it past Roa. End of story.

The sheer normality of the end – without a doping scandal, or an unfair red card, or any such off-field event – left fans in a speechless limbo. "We have paid the price of arrogance," concluded one commentator in an outburst of cold reason. People in cafes just stared at the screen, digesting it all. The drizzle kept on falling, and what had looked like Milan on Tuesday night turned slowly into Hartlepool.

The local kiosk owner was happy, or at least she said she was. "Now we can get back to normal life," she clucked before a queue of dog-faced customers minutes after the finale in Marseille. And normal Argentina did return: Batistuta told reporters that it wasn't his fault, that "I did my job"; politicians started plotting to rewrite the constitution, and the old footballing gripes flowered. Both the press and an unusually sane Maradona blamed Passarella for abandoning tradition and the team's "historical mandate" on the pitch. It was, they argued, an Argentina made in Italy and not in shanty-land.

The rest of the World Cup was watched with a sort of exhausted indifference, normal news programmes returned and the team came back home to be greeted by 300 hyperventilating teenage girls. Pictures of Parisian streets crammed with victorious fans only served to raise some ironic asides, providing one of the very few occasions on which Argentina allows itself a knowing smile: the happiness, they knew, would not last.

A day before the final, one paper published a short story about an Argentinian philosopher who decides to support England as a thought experiment. At first, it proves hard for him not to cheer Argentina's first goal. But by the end, things have changed. He is desperate for England to win on penalties. Days after the match, he is seen roaming the streets of Buenos Aires, his face contorted with pain, murmuring to himself repeatedly one simple reprimand: "Fucking *Argentinos*, fucking *Argentinos*."

call me Mr Bora

Osasu Obayiuwana

Philippe Troussier was standing in a hotel lobby shortly after being sacked by the Nigerian FA, having piloted the national team through the qualifiers for the 1998 World Cup. He was in no doubt about the qualities a foreign trainer needed to survive the minefields of Nigerian football. "Only a cowboy can coach Nigeria," he shrugged.

True to form, the NFA went out and found one. Bora Milutinovic, the eccentric Serb whose public persona brings to mind Jerry Lewis in *The Nutty Professor*, was initially hailed by the Nigerian media as "a World Cup coach capable of bringing the trophy back home". But it didn't take too long for him to be dumped in the doghouse. The 5-1 loss to Holland on June 5th, following poor results against Yugoslavia and the Swiss First Division side Grasshoppers, was almost the last straw.

"Our game against Holland was terrible. I don't see why Bora is still in charge. We are in for a bollocking if he takes us to the World

Cup," said Dele Momodu, publisher of the London-based Nigerian society magazine, *Ovation*. Milutinovic would indeed have gone, but for an act of fate – the sudden death of the country's dictator, General Sani Abacha. Abacha had accepted the request of Daniel Amokachi and other senior members of the team to fire the Serbian coach and replace him with Jo Bonfrere, the Dutchman who led the Eagles to the gold medal at the 1996 Olympics, but his demise on June 8th left Milutinovic hanging on to the reins.

While the press held Milutinovic responsible for the poor friendly results, they also had the country's football officials in their sights, citing numerous instances of their bungling. The chairman of the Nigerian FA, Abdulmumuni Aminu, in turn blamed the press for events on the field. Once the squad arrived in France he decided to bar all journalists from the team's headquarters at Chateau de Bellinglise, 45 minutes outside Paris, saying: "We have had enough of the disturbances in the camp which have contributed to the recent dismal results."

But that did not stop the *Post Express*, one of Nigeria's leading dailies, from detailing the stormy session that took place on Wednesday June 10th, three days before the Eagles' opening game against Spain. **Aminu Offers To Quit** screamed its headline. The paper revealed that the players had gone on strike the Monday before, refusing to train until their outstanding bonuses had been paid. Aminu was literally begging the players to believe that all would be settled, purportedly offering to resign "if you [the players] think I am the problem".

Even on the morning of the Spain match Onochie Anibeze, sports editor of the *Vanguard*, had no qualms about laying into Milutinovic. "As far as I am concerned, he has not shown himself to be a coach that can handle our team. He may have been a big name in Mexico, Costa Rica and the USA, but Nigeria is a different thing entirely. He is just a guy that saw an opportunity to make a lot of money coaching us and would be off to the next job at the first sign of trouble."

That afternoon, after Fernando Hierro scored Spain's first goal, I looked around at the despondent faces of the 40 or so Nigerian journalists in the press box. They were preparing to fry Bora, but they had to hold fire after the Eagles' dramatic turn around. "There's nothing like a win to keep people happy is there?" said a triumphant Milutinovic, as he entered the media room, wearing a white *agbada* (a traditional Nigerian dress) as the Nigerian journalists, led by Onochie and Dave Enechukwu, sports editor of the *Post Express*, staged a victory dance. Other journalists asked for translations of the songs they were singing in Yoruba and Ibo, two of Nigeria's three main languages. Seeing such gloating over his misfortune was almost too much to bear for the Spanish coach Javier Clemente, who seemed on the point of turning on his heel and heading back to the dressing room.

But the respite was to be short for Milutinovic. Although the Eagles won the subsequent match against Bulgaria, few were satisfied with the 1-0 scoreline. "This team is playing with no sense of purpose. They've scored one goal and they think it's all over," fumed Muyiwa Daniel of the *National Concord*, a paper owned by the late Moshood Abiola, the multi-millionaire businessman and winner of Nigeria's 1993 presidential elections who was subsequently placed under arrest by the Abacha regime. Daniel had no intention of giving Milutinovic an easy time at the press conference that followed: "Why is your team so arrogant? They scored a goal and let the Bulgarians do the playing!" he hollered as the Serb ignored him and pressed on with multilingual responses to questions offered by journalists from other countries.

Writing in his popular column in the daily newspaper, the *Punch*, Abimbola Akinloye made his preference for Bonfrere as coach quite clear. "The NFA decided to pick the wrong man as coach. They say Bora is a World Cup coach, but what did he achieve with the three teams that he took to the World Cup before us? Getting to the second round is no big deal when we have the potential to win. I think the level of expectation is overwhelming him. He has never had to cope with this type of pressure."

Bora, usually skilled at getting the media on his side, was unable to charm his way around the Nigerian press pack. They constantly raised objections to his working methods and defensive tactics, which did not seem to be bringing the best out of the team's wealth of talent. It came as no surprise when the press conference that followed the team's unexpected 3-1 loss to Paraguay degenerated into a farce. Taye Ige, a writer with a Nigerian news magazine, the *Week*, asked questions that called Milutinovic's competence into doubt, provoking a fiery response: "For you, my friend, I want you to call me Mr Bora, not Bora. Show me some respect. I am proud of my achievement with this team. After all, I placed first in the group of death. I don't have anything to prove until we play our second round opponent." Milutinovic refused to take any more questions from the Nigerian media that day.

Back home in Lagos, Godwin Dudu-Orumen, a lawyer turned television football pundit, was following the unfolding debacle with keen interest. On his popular television show, *The Best of Football*, he had predicted that the Eagles' participation at France 98 would end in disaster, comments which made him the target of what he says were "vitriolic attacks from the media and the general public".

"Many people were surprised that I decided to stay in Nigeria during the tournament, rather than go to France," he said. "But with what I had seen go on, I was almost certain that we were destined to fail. I only gave my candid opinion about the selection of players for the World Cup, but people were just not ready to hear it." Orumen criticised the exclusion from the squad of the VfB Stuttgart striker Jonathan Akpoborie and questioned the inclusion of the veteran Rashidi Yekini. "Akpoborie had helped Stuttgart reach the finals of the European Cup-Winners Cup and had scored a decent number of goals for the national team. As far as I am concerned, the lad was excluded from the team because some influential Yoruba members of the Football Association [the area of Nigeria from which Yekini comes] wanted their own man in the team. It was only after we lost that people realised what I had been saying."

Orumen's allegations were given credence by an exposé in the *Vanguard.* **REVEALED: Bora Invited Akpoborie – But Eagles Mafia Rules Him Out** ran their headline. Onochie Anibeze, the writer of the story, claimed that a cabal of players had opposed the Bundesliga player's inclusion in the team, threatening to kick up a fuss if they did not get their way.

Despite the troubles tearing the Nigerian team apart, the media's previews of their second round game against Denmark were upbeat. They reasoned that a Danish team that had struggled to beat Saudi Arabia, barely managed a draw against South Africa and crumbled to a French side that apparently had no striker, could not pose any problems for the Nigerians who had beaten two European teams to top their group. The 3-1 loss to Paraguay was a blip, they argued, because Milutinovic had put out a severely weakened side.

Even Bora's detractors could not have expected the 4-1 thrashing handed out by the Danes at the Stade de France. And as soon as the game ended, Football Association officials, who had previously kept their distance from the press, began to sing like canaries. In an attempt to put the blame on the players, Sani Toro, the NFA's secretary-general, told the press that the players had demanded a payment of $10,000 per man before the game, threatening to boycott the match if their demands were not met.

"These players are greedy and unpatriotic," fumed Richard Asiegbu, a broadcaster with Nigeria's national radio station, who presented a daily World Cup show from Paris. He did not spare the players on his programme. "Why should they be demanding money when their thoughts should be on the match? It is sad that the FA succumbed to blackmail. It shows the calibre of people that run football in Nigeria."

But the answer to that query came from another *Vanguard* story that hit the streets days after the Eagles' unceremonious exit. **Money! Money!! Money!!! Eagles Explain Action Against NFA**. It was an interview with one of the players, who declined to be identified, spilling the beans on the mass corruption that he said

was going on among football officials. "The NFA had said that our qualification bonus and other outstanding allowance would be paid during the match against Germany in Cologne [played in April]. They did not pay us and claimed that they did not have the money. But somebody from FIFA told us that a top official of the Football Association collected Nigeria's World Cup qualification payment from FIFA on the grounds that 'we are going to pay our players with it'." According to the report, the unnamed Nigerian official collected the sum of $750,000 in cash from FIFA in Zurich, but none of this money reached the players.

The maladministration surrounding Nigeria's World Cup misadventure prompted the Ajax Amsterdam star Sunday Oliseh to announce his retirement from international football at the (official) age of 23. It was a decision that may be copied by several of his European-based colleagues, fed up with the greed and incompetence of FA officials. Nigeria may still harbour ambitions of upsetting the balance of power in world football, but first they will have to get past their toughest opponent: their own FA.

crumbs of comfort

Justin McCurry

After four and a half hours

of football, and with just a single goal and no points to show for their efforts, the Japanese team returned home from France dreaming of 2002, when they will at least gain automatic qualification. But brief as it was, Japan's first foray into the World Cup finals was by no means as disastrous as the statistics suggest. On the contrary, it left a lasting impression on domestic attitudes toward the game that are bound to endure until 2002 and beyond. It turned a nation largely ignorant of football into one that had been exposed to the full gamut of emotions the game has to offer.

Before France 98, Japan had achieved only minor successes in international competition, having won a bronze medal at the 1968 Mexico Olympics and the Asian Cup under Dutch coach Hans Ooft in 1992. Moreover, until 1993, the country's top footballers were still amateurs, playing for corporate teams in the old Japan Football League.

Such an ignominious international record makes the sheer scale and intensity of the build-up to France all the more surprising. It also makes it difficult to explain why, on the back of warm-up defeats against Mexico and Yugoslavia, and draws against Paraguay and the Czech Republic, Japan went into their first match against Argentina with the full backing of an expectant nation. In fact, the form books had been dispensed with ever since November 1997, when a golden goal against Iran in Johor Bahru, Malaysia, secured Japan's place in France and turned both scorer Masayuki Okano and newly appointed coach Takeshi Okada into national heroes.

There are several reasons for this. Football itself was a novelty, a visually attractive, simple game, for a nation of ready-made sports fans more accustomed to the tactical intricacies of professional baseball and the rituals and conservatism of sumo wrestling. The World Cup also offered a means of escape from the dual torments of Japan's long and humid rainy season, and the worst recession since the end of the Second World War. Above all, there was the feeling that Japan was damn well going to make the most of reaching the world's most visible sporting event.

For younger fans, male and female, the game offers unpredictability and an opportunity for unashamed exuberance not often afforded them in their daily lives. For them, the finals were proof that for every uninspiring, immutable baseball coach, there is a Takeshi Okada who was not only prepared to drop from his squad the most famous footballer in the country, but who also had the temerity to predict that his team would qualify for the last 16.

It showed them that there is an alternative to the servility of up-and-coming sumo wrestlers, eager to thank their supporters with promises to do better – sports stars can also behave like Hidetoshi Nakata, the (briefly) orange-mopped pin-up boy who has no hesitation in accusing team-mates of lacking the intelligence to play successfully alongside him. The same Nakata, minutes after the team qualified for the tournament, chastised the millions of fans watching back home for not showing the same interest in the wilting J-League as they had in international fixtures. Nakata's comments, however, did not deter the *Ultras Nippon* from making the trip to Europe in their tens of thousands.

That so many made it to France is surprising considering that a ticketing scandal threatened to spoil Japan's dream before a ball had been kicked. As the team's date with Argentina in Toulouse approached, major travel agencies began reporting a severe shortage of tickets via hapless representatives, who were often sent to dispatch the bad news to already excitable fans at Tokyo's Narita airport. The agents bravely admitted that of the 14,700 tickets promised for the Argentina clash, only 2,200 had turned up. In a display of impromptu risk-taking rarely seen in a people more used to round-the-clock mollycoddling on package tours, more than 11,000 supporters went to France for the first group match anyway. Judging by the scenes inside the stadiums at all three matches, they found the locals, via not-so-local touts, more than willing to meet demand with a steady supply of tickets, albeit at scandalous prices.

The ticket fiasco brought out rebelliousness in the most unlikely quarters. One 34-year-old woman, after being informed at the airport that her tickets had failed to materialise, said: "If we don't get the tickets soon, we're going to take the tour co-ordinator hostage – but we won't kill him." In the end, only two-thirds of the tickets for the three group games turned up, but that did not stop an estimated 35,000 travelling to France, including some who had done the almost unthinkable in Japan and quit their jobs to follow the team for the entire period of their involvement.

Okada, meanwhile, was having problems with team selection, something that would ultimately prove to be his undoing. Days before the team was due to move to its base camp in Aix-les-Bains, he dropped a bombshell. Unceremoniously dumped from his 22-man squad was Kazuyoshi "Kazu" Miura, along with the popular-but-past-it Tsuyoshi Kitazawa and the school-age Daisuke Ichikawa. Rather than take a chance on the 31-year-old Miura, whose goalscoring form had dipped considerably the previous year, Okada opted instead to build his attack around the 21-year-old Yokohama Marinos striker Shoji Jo.

As the only Japanese to have played in Italy's Serie A (for Genoa in 1994-95) and with 54 goals in 86 international appearances, there were compelling reasons for Kazu's inclusion. His disappointment at being left out was such that he was sent home early by Okada, who feared his depression would rub off on the rest of the squad. Okada's brave decision upset one or two back home as well. The Japan Football Association reportedly received more than 1,000 threatening phone calls from angry fans within hours of the announcement, and police were sent to watch the Okada family home.

The press, too, seemed to feel that Okada's much-lauded determination to break the mould and run the team according to his rules had gone awry. Sports columnist Jeremy Walker wrote in the English-language *Daily Yomiuri*: "The nation has thrown a sentimental arm around the shoulder of the fallen hero. Okada has made a big mistake in discarding King Kazu and, deep down inside, he knows it." Kazu surfaced at Narita Airport sporting a peroxide blonde hairdo courtesy of a salon in Milan. He proceeded to tell reporters he would continue playing at club level, but in a most un-Japanese manner admitted that he could not "just take it on the chin".

Exclusive rights to all 64 World Cup games had been awarded to NHK, Japan's equivalent of the BBC. NHK overcame the problem of the seven-hour time difference by repeating all the games the following day. The station must have dispatched its most able negotiators to France before the tournament: all three of Japan's group matches kicked off late in the afternoon, two of them at the weekend, meaning they would be broadcast live in Japan just in time for fans fresh from work, day-trips or early-evening drinking sessions.

Some of the commercial stations, which were allowed to show short highlights in their daily digests, opted for an approach that confirmed Japan's long absence from the international game at the highest level had left its pundits, as well as its players, short of some of the essential skills. Many approached the Argentina game as if it were a mathematical conundrum that could be easily overcome provided the correct formula were applied. The impression was given that the Argentinian players would oblige by responding in almost exactly the way they had done in an endless stream of televised simulations presided over by former professionals who really should have known better.

One televised computer simulation declared Japan 2-1 winners in a match against Argentina. While the programme's guests, few of whom were from the football world, cooed at this remarkable upset, it was pointed out almost as an afterthought that the simulation was merely one of ten carried out under different conditions, and that in fact, Argentina had emerged victorious in seven. The weirdest simulation of the bunch was performed by 22 ants –11 representing Argentina and 11 Japan – who "played" with a crumb painted to resemble a football.

On the day of the big game, television stations reminded viewers, as if anyone really needed reminding, of the number of hours left to endure before kick-off. References to the game were invariably prefaced with the words "historic" or "history-making", a pattern that would continue until that first World Cup goal against Jamaica. Before the kick-off NHK hosted an evening of pre-match football chat and live feeds from groups of supporters at venues around the country holding as many as 1,000 blue-shirted fans seated before giant screens.

Away from the fray, the nation's entertainment business was given the night off. In Shinjuku, one of Tokyo's busiest districts, normally bustling restaurants had emptied by the 9.30pm kick-off time and even the local "pink" trade, a collection of massage parlours and the like, was reduced to offering special discounts.

Almost two-thirds of all households in the Tokyo area – more than nine million people – watched the 1-0 defeat by Argentina. The national figure hovered around 60 per cent, even increasing slightly for the games against Croatia and Jamaica. The Tokyo figure was the sixth highest for a sporting event since 1962. (First place is still held, incredibly, by the women's volleyball final between Japan and the Soviet Union at the 1964 Tokyo Olympics.)

Toshikatsu Kawaguchi's heroics in goal won him high praise in the following morning's newspapers. **The Best Goalkeeper In The World**, proclaimed the *Hochi Shimbun*. **We Fought The Brave Fight**, ran a front-page headline in *Sports Nippon*. But the feeling that Japan had come so close to upsetting the two-time world champions was best summed up by the *Daily Sport*'s **Almost! Almost! Almost!** Japan would earn a point against Croatia before pulling off that historic first World Cup win against Jamaica, they predicted.

Worried by the failure in front of goal of striking duo Masashi Nakayama and Shoji Jo, who had failed to find the net in seven consecutive games, sections of the press called for the inclusion against Croatia of Okano, the hero of the qualifying rounds. Instead, Jo and Nakayama started, with Okano being given just 30 minutes to turn the game around. The 1-0 defeat marked a turning point for frustrated fans who had hitherto been content to leave team selection in Okada's hands. Many questioned the coach's defensive line-up and asked why Brazilian-born attacker Wagner Lopes was not being given more time on the field. When Argentina sealed Japan's fate the following day with a 5-0 trouncing of Jamaica, it became clear that Okada would resign after the team's final group match.

The Jo-Nakayama partnership survived to start the Jamaica game, a decision that flew in the face of advice proffered by media tacticians. Calls grew for the inclusion of 18-year-old Urawa Reds midfielder Shinji Ono, who, the *Nikkan Sports* newspaper predicted, would score that "historic" first goal. The advice was lost on Okada, who only gave Ono his chance with less than ten minutes of the game remaining. Yet another live feed showed Ono's mother sitting in front of a giant screen, face hidden behind hands, no doubt wondering along with the rest of the nation why her son had not been brought on, say, 80 minutes earlier.

Japan finally ended their goal drought with a close-range strike from Nakayama. The only problem was that fellow first-timers Jamaica had already scored two historic goals of their own. Most match reports the following day were reflective, their contents ranging from mild criticism of the coach's tactics, to praise for his achievements in getting the team to France in the first place. The *Gendai Sports* was less forgiving, asking whether Japanese football was indeed the worst in the world, and questioning the right of Japan and South Korea to co-host the 2002 tournament.

Fans, too, fresh from their three-week crash course in football punditry, seemed to have lost faith in Okada, as well as one or two of his first-choice players. One told the *Shukan Taishu* weekly magazine: "I feel betrayed by Okada. The three games leave us with nothing to remember. Throughout this whole World Cup, the only decisive thing Okada did was to cut Kazu." And that, it seemed, was at the heart of the team's problems. If only Japan had been able to take with them a striker with the finishing power of Kazu, or even the man himself.

On his return to Japan, Jo was unceremoniously splattered with water by a disgruntled fan, although one dissenter in a welcoming committee of more than 1,000 at Narita airport hardly suggested widespread disaffection. In spite of the nasty faxes sent to television stations and newspapers, as well as several threatening phone calls to his parents' home, the 21-year-old Jo knows that his international career is far from over.

It is too early to tell whether the momentum and interest created by France 98 can be maintained until the next finals. Much will depend on the standard and entertainment value of the J-League. Early signs suggest the World Cup has had an impact that goes some way towards justifying the hype. Japan's participation introduced the world's first potential Asian star in Hidetoshi Nakata, who has since signed for Serie A club Perugia. Nakata is unlike any Japanese sportsman in recent memory in his self-confidence – which many wrongly interpret as arrogance – and his dislike of the mindless platitudes that are the stock-in-trade of other Japanese sports stars. A successful debut season in Italy would help advance the education of fans back home and will probably deepen, rather than dissipate, interest in the domestic game, in the same way Japanese pitcher Hideo Nomo's move to the US Major League prefaced a surge of interest in baseball.

The need to export home-grown talent was a recurring theme in many of the post mortems offered by the press and league officials. Even the chairman of the J-League, Saburo Kawabuchi, told one reporter he would love to see more Japanese playing for European clubs. Others talked of the need for players to "get out of the greenhouse" and expose themselves to a "harsher environment".

Another significant indicator of football's hold on the Japanese public may be the development of interest among women. A glance at the Japanese contingent at any of the three group matches in France confirmed they are a very sizeable minority of the game's devotees. Since the J-League's inception, young Japanese women, many of them single and with considerable disposable income, have been the target of a vigorous marketing campaign. Football-related goods, from posters of the team's more attractive members, to leisurewear, to the cuddly mascots representing each J-League team, were without doubt designed with the young female consumer in mind. The Ultras Nippon counts several women among its most committed members, and more are attracted by the idol-like status enjoyed by some of the team's stars, notably Nakata, Jo and Kawaguchi.

However, young women are a demographic group renowned for their faddishness in Japan, and it remains to be seen whether they will develop and sustain an interest in the game for the game's sake – although the mixed fortunes of the J-League over the past five years suggest the same can be said to some extent of all Japanese fans, regardless of gender.

Yet despite such uncertainties and the relatively poor showing of the team in France, the World Cup will surely prove to have been a watershed in the penetration of football into Japan's national consciousness. The upper house elections at the end of July provided an unlikely illustration of this. The ruling Liberal Democratic Party suffered badly at the hands of the Democratic Party of Japan, whose supporters canvassed in the streets dressed in football shirts. Soon after the election, the Democratic leader, Naoto Kan, declared on television that the Japanese people had shown Prime Minister Ryutaro Hashimoto "the red card".

Kan's decision to use the footballing metaphor is an indication of why he is seen as someone who moves with the times. Had he used similar language just several months earlier, few Japanese of voting age would have understood what he was talking about. Not only was the comment cleverly timed, it turned out to be correct – Hashimoto left the field of play only days later.

wake up, please

Mark Brownlow

So that was it, was it?

All that waiting, wondering if it really was going to be something special. And what did we get? A long period of fairly boring foreplay, a brief moment of excitement at the climax, then a frustrating feeling of mild dissatisfaction when it was over. No fireworks or stars in our eyes. No second-round cracker against Brazil. Just two scrappy draws, an honourable defeat and a rapid exit.

But there were no real villains, no heroes either, just the fact that the team just didn't quite have what it takes. As one paper put it, they occupied their usual position of being neither a success nor a failure, the 200 fans who turned up at the airport being "too few to make them heroes, but too many to make them losers". The Austrian World Cup campaign 1998 – we came, we saw, we went home again.

Anyone watching the final qualification match in Vienna might have been forgiven for expecting much more from France 98. A full

stadium, ecstatic fans, football euphoria throughout the nation. Stuck between east and west, and with a history far more illustrious than its likely future, Austria often turns to its sporting stars for a sense of importance in the modern world. Even the chancellor, Viktor Klima, became a football fan over the summer, claiming he got so excited at matches he was "a danger to those near me".

After Austria qualified, comparisons were being made with the *Wunderteam*, which travelled to the 1934 World Cup as favourites before losing in the semi-final. But it was left to the serious commentators to remind us that while the *Wunderteam* thrashed the likes of France, Germany and Italy in the years prior to the tournament, the current lot had taken out Belarus, Latvia and Estonia.

Regardless, Austrian fans were actually looking forward to France, rather than worrying about potential global humiliation, as has often been the case in the past. And they had a right to be optimistic. There was a strong spirit in the team, which was built around a core of top-class players earning their money abroad; Toni Polster (Köln, now Mönchengladbach) up front, Michael Konsel (Roma) in goal, Wolfgang Feiersinger (Dortmund) at the back. And in the middle Bremen's Andi Herzog – the "toe of the nation", a man whose injuries kept the back pages of the dailies busy for weeks. He never disclosed which foot was affected until the eventual operation was over, which presumably meant that defenders stomped on both feet, just to be sure.

Team manager Prohaska's reservations about making the second round were swept away by a wave of enthusiasm that grew faster than Paul Gascoigne's bar bill. By the time the first preparation match came round, everyone was looking forward to a goal feast. After all, the opponents – Hungary – had just been thrashed by Yugoslavia in the qualification play-offs. A goal feast it was – five goals, three of them for the wrong team.

There were a few furrowed brows around the stadium, some thoughtful "hmmms" in the press box. But judgement was reserved for the next match, at home to the US. The team promised to make up for the Hungary result... and promptly lost 3-0. By the end of the match, the Austrian fans were cheering every US pass. Prohaska admitted the team might have lost all the goodwill built up in qualification and, as fairweather sponsors thought about jumping ship, the commercial manager accused the players of ruining business. Later that night, Polster was filmed dancing with samba girls at the night-club launch of his new book. Nice one Anton.

The next day, one newspaper commentary lead with the headline **Wake Up, Please** – directed at the fans, not the players. The boundless optimism fostered by a near-perfect qualification was shattered. Reality is fine if you support Brazil, but if reality means watching a team of workhorses getting torn apart by a virgin soccer nation like the US, then forgive us our dreams. Worse, the team spirit, the single most important factor in the qualification triumphs, started to wither. There were rumours that the home-based players were irritated by all the media attention given to Polster and Herzog.

Polster himself, who repeatedly states the importance of not moaning and getting on with things, got on with moaning about Ivica Vastic, his striking partner. Everyone pointed fingers at an appalling defence. Manager Prohaska defended his players, but his heart wasn't in it. A scrappy win against Tunisia and a 6-0 victory over a ten-man Liechtenstein failed to give the necessary reassurance. Still, for fans and media alike, there was always the comforting thought that performances in friendlies and performances in the World Cup are two different things. So, armed with their own cook (there were "problems with the desserts" during a previous training camp), it was on to Bordeaux, for the big one. Expectations were (still) high.

Austria's state-owned television channel, ORF, went the whole hog for the tournament, flushed by their recent success at the Nagano Winter Olympics. Austrian TV's main advantage during any international event is that Vienna is a city with a large United

Nations presence, so there is always a handy group of Japanese, Chileans or Moroccans on hand to be filmed cheering their team on in some *Gasthaus*. Nevertheless, ORF and the World Cup is like rain on your wedding day; it's not going to completely spoil the occasion, but it does put a real dampener on things. There is no private terrestrial competition (a situation mirrored in Europe only by Albania), so viewers without cable TV don't know any better.

ORF's two guest stars for the tournament were Josef Hickersberger, for pre- and post-match comment, and Hans Krankl, as co-commentator for the key matches. Hickersberger took a pretty dreary national team to the 1990 World Cup, but is best known for his last match in charge, the infamous defeat against the Faroe Islands later that year. Dull as bread at first appearances, he impressed with his analytical skills and realistic appraisal of the Austrian performances.

Krankl is the golden boy of Austrian football. Still revered for the two goals which defeated Germany at the 1978 World Cup, he tends to speak with his heart and not his head, which further endears him to viewers, if not to purists. Like most ORF sports reporters he is prone to stereotyping. There are no Scottish players, just "bravehearts", Colin Hendry has achieved icon-like status as "the blond Hun" and the Brazilians could do a passable imitation of Wimbledon on a bad day and still be described as "samba magic".

On the first day of the competition, the best-selling Austrian paper *Die Kronen Zeitung* headlined with **Austrians Avoid Risk**. The words referred to a survey showing that workers would prefer lower pay in return for more job security, but it turned out to be a fairly accurate description of Austria's tactics in their opening 1-1 draw against Cameroon. One Croatian paper described the two teams as having "tortured the ball". Franz Beckenbauer, who often feels the need to comment on Austrian football, described the team as having played with "no brain", whereas captain Polster thought they were "all heart". It's doubtful they meant quite the same thing.

But the general euphoria over Polster's late equaliser enabled everyone to ignore the fact that it was what one national daily called "the worst, slowest, tactically and technically most inferior game of the tournament to date".

Polster himself described the goal as a proper reply to all those who had begun to question whether he deserved his place in the team, paradoxically adding: "I don't have anything to prove." Herzog was perhaps the biggest disappointment. Hurt more by his own performance than the (relatively gentle) media criticism, he removed himself from public view, refused to give interviews and played the next two games as a substitute.

By the time the next match arrived, disaster had struck in my own household. A desperate phone call, a business offer "you can't refuse", and I found myself watching the Austria-Chile match in Turkey. Thank God for Eurosport. For the first (and probably the last time), downtown Ankara echoed to the cry of "Ivi-ca Vas-tic!" as the naturalised Croat scored another last-gasp equaliser for Austria after coming on as a substitute. Before the game many newspapers and fans had been calling for Vastic, to bring in some speed and creativity. Vastic has godlike status in Graz, where he led Sturm to their first championship last season, and is widely regarded as the best (and best-looking) footballer in the domestic league. But he has never really won over the hearts of the fans outside Graz, and was obviously moved when the fans at the Chile match started chanting his name.

Nevertheless, it was another dour, defensive Austrian performance – appalling to watch, but a reasonable result. However, delight at another saved point was slowly tempered by the knowledge that the team would probably have to beat Italy to qualify for the next round. Much of the post-match debate revolved around Salas's goal for Chile, when the ball barely crossed the line. Goalkeeper Konsel was adamant that it had not, but even in-depth analysis using the hi-tech Lego football pitch in the ORF studio failed to establish the facts either way.

Two days before the decisive match against Italy, ORF, Krankl and most of the country celebrated the 20th anniversary of that 3-2 defeat of Germany in Argentina (in which Berti Vogts scored an own goal). If it was intended to remind the current players that anything is possible, they failed to take the lesson to heart. At least there was respectability in the 2-1 defeat and a whole-hearted effort, even if the Austrian goal came yet again in time added on (a Herzog penalty). The sight of an Italian defender desperately hacking the ball into the stands to relieve the pressure on his beleaguered defence was one of the few memories Austrian fans could look back on with pleasure.

Polster, once again following his "don't moan, get on with it" maxim to the letter, moaned in full afterwards, mostly about referee Paul Durkin. Stripped of their French expense accounts, the ORF team flapped around like a blind octopus, desperately seeking someone or something to blame. Visibly irritated at having to pack up their bags and head back to Vienna, they vented their frustration on Prohaska, who was blamed for not being adventurous enough in team selection. Back home, the reaction was more favourable. After relatively undistinguished performances in the last World Cup campaigns, the team had, at least, not disgraced themselves. After each of the three matches the same comment could be heard around the country: "We could have won that." But we didn't.

With no team of their own to support, most Austrians remained neutral for the rest of the tournament, except of course when Germany were playing. Austrian TV usually feels obliged to transfer its support to our northern neighbours once local interest in any football competition is lost. As a consequence, they inflict Bayern Munich v Gothenburg on us on Wednesday nights, when we could be watching Manchester United play Juventus. This preference is not shared by much of the Austrian population, however, who the spent the rest of the World Cup enjoying Germany's troubles.

The relationship with Germany, like so many components of Austria's national identity, is a paradox. Germans are hated and loved, encouraged to spend their holidays in the Alps, yet lampooned when they do so. It is a popular misconception in Europe that Austria and Germany are two branches of the same tree, but people tend to forget that Austria also had an empire to call their own until the First World War and, but for the period of Nazi rule after 1938, Austria and Germany have never been one country.

For many an Austrian football supporter there is nothing better than seeing the national team beat their often patronising neighbours. Indeed, playing Germany at football seems to be the most efficient means of focusing the minds of Austrians on their own identity – after the 1978 World Cup victory market research organisations recorded a steep increase in positive responses to the question: Is Austria a nation?

The Germany-Croatia game added a further geopolitical element to this conflict. Like Germany, Austria took in more refugees from the civil war in Yugoslavia than other EU states and there are still relatively large populations of Serbs, Croats and Bosnians in the country, particularly in Vienna. While there is little overt racism towards them, the far-right Freedom Party of Jörg Haider has the strongest electoral support of any similar movement in Europe, and it would be fair to say that refugees from former Yugoslavia and Austrians have yet to find much common ground.

But what bonds there are have been largely forged by football. As well as Vastic, other exports such as Otto Baric (ex-manager of Salzburg, now in Linz) and Ivica Osim (manager of Sturm Graz) have brought international success to Austrian clubs, while the children of refugees and guest workers have already helped Austria become junior street soccer world champions.

To make things more complicated, Austria has severely tangled historic ties to Croatia, which was part of the Habsburg empire before the creation of Yugoslavia, and tends to use that fact to emphasise its "Europeanness" in contrast to the Serbs, whose imperial masters were the Ottoman Turks. So when Germany met Croatia in France, it might have been a tricky one to call, but most Austrians had no difficulty in identifying with the small former colony to the south rather than the giant to the north.

Thousands packed in front of large video screens, almost all willing Croatia to win. After the game the mild-mannered liberal newspaper *Der Standard* expressed the feelings of many in a scathing attack on the German team, saying their defeat had "removed a nightmare from the World Cup" and accusing them of "creative minimalism". In the greatest insult of them all, the paper claimed that "Matthäus is even slower than Polster". Some consolation, but not much.

So what remains now that the party is over? The realisation that it probably was enough, after all, just to have qualified; the knowledge that a new, younger team will have to emerge now that Polster, Pfeffer, Feiersinger and Pfeifenberger are all over 30; the acceptance that life is hard for a football team from a country of just eight million (damn those Danes for screwing up that excuse); and the pleasure of knowing that the World Cup is always closely followed by another successful season for the skiers. That Hermann Maier – now there's a man who really knows how to crash out of a competition.

the off day

Adriaan Grijns

Brazil are losing 1-0

as I get into the taxi that will take me to the place where I am supposed to watch them crush Denmark. I wonder whether the others have arrived already, considering the time it takes me to get to Serge's house. Traffic jams in Rio de Janeiro between 3 and 4pm on some Tuesdays in June and July 1998 have reportedly been the worst in the city's history.

Economic activity stops during matches of the *Seleção* (national team). At the law firm where I work, Brazil-Scotland was watched at the office, starting at 12.30pm, and analysed for the rest of the afternoon. For Brazil-Morocco, we were allowed by the partners to leave at 3pm. The office manager disagreed and kicked us out at 2.30, but it was still hard to make it on time. Now it's Denmark, another game kicking off in the evening in France, which means the late afternoon for us.

People are driving extremely nervously, and three lanes quickly become five. Those who have to travel for more than two hours to get home have stayed in bars to watch. I ask the taxi driver why he is not watching the match. "I did for two minutes until the first goal, then I jumped into my car and drove away furiously," he says. The radio is off. But moments of deep depression can rapidly turn into moments of utter joy in Brazil: a girl in a tight dress crosses the road with a smile and causes hundreds of cars to abruptly respect the traffic lights. My driver cheers loudly: "Luck can change so easily in life."

His point is emphasised a few minutes later when Bebeto equalises, as we learn from the sudden explosion of noise from hooting cars, fireworks going off, and people in bars rushing into the street. Now my taxi driver wants to stop and watch the game. I tell him to carry on and get me there as quickly as possible. He looks at me in disbelief but complies.

Once seated in front of the TV with beers and snacks, all the magic of the *Copa do Mundo* suddenly seems to fade away. All the streets festooned with yellow and green, the jingles on television, the advertisements with Ronaldo ("The Best Player on the Planet") playing football with kids dressed as animals in a Parmalat forest, or the one with Roberto Carlos's flying slipper circling the globe, the lotteries and the rest of the paraphernalia, all suddenly seem exactly what they are: diversions. Something is wrong with this *Seleção*.

But whatever it is, it has been left anxiously undiscussed. After the defeat by Norway, the media happily shifted attention to the nation's mourning over the tragic death of country music star Leandro, the former tomato picker from the inland state of Goiás, and one half of Brazil's immensely popular duo Leandro and Leonardo (coach Mario Zagallo's promise to dedicate victory over Norway to Leandro was wryly remembered). Nevertheless, there are a few cracks in the facade. The papers noted that Brazil had not lost a single match on any of the four occasion they had won the World Cup – 1958, 1962, 1970 and 1994. Many football fans I talked to in Rio said they had already lost confidence in a Brazil without Romário (although polls in São Paulo showed overwhelming approval of the decision to send him home).

Others cling to Ronaldo's promise that he would score at least 13 goals – one for each member of his family and friends gathered in the house he rented for £15,000 a month near the village of Ozoires, where the squad stayed throughout most of the tournament. With only four scored so far, and a maximum of three games to go, this would entail some impressive victories over the next few opponents. People love this kind of spectacular prediction. However, Ronaldo again does not score. Instead Rivaldo – who is later accused of not passing to Ronaldo – takes Brazil by the hand and they finally dispose of Denmark 3-2. To celebrate we have the choice between samba parties, beach dancing or fights between drunk Flamengo fans and the rest.

The game was Brazil's best so far in the tournament according to the newspapers, which are full of promises that the team has finally found the right path. Promises are important in Brazil. Romário promised to win the Cup in 1994, and did so (on his own, according to his version). Now everyone is promising everyone else the *Penta* (the fifth title). Brazil beat Holland too, and the smiling faces on television conclude that "although the real final hasn't been played yet, the dream is coming true".

But the dream did not come true. The real final was lost and the World Cup did not come back to Brazil as promised. The nation felt cheated. For many Brazilians the World Cup did not end on the day of the final. Clearly, higher powers had prevented Brazil from winning and the culprit had to be found. Certain obvious candidates suggested themselves: Nike; Ricardo Teixeira, the powerful president of the Brazilian FA (and former son-in-law of João Havelange); Lídio Toledo, the physician of the *Seleção*, who came under heavy suspicion for his decision to send Romário home with an "injury" – *o baixinho* (shorty) was seen playing football on the beach a few days later.

The day after the final, most papers hardly mentioned the score, concentrating instead on the mysterious attack suffered by Ronaldo earlier in the day and its effect on the other players. Still nobody

knows exactly what happened, but from the information given by Roberto Carlos I surmise the following: Roberto Carlos and Ronaldo are lying on their beds in the room they share; Ronaldo is reading *Playboy* and Roberto Carlos is watching Eurosport. Suddenly Ronaldo starts to moan and to drool. Roberto Carlos gets embarrassed and asks for some privacy. At that moment Ronaldo's tongue is already halfway down his throat and the final is lost. Versions from other players are slightly contradictory: they say that it was not Ronaldo but Roberto Carlos himself who was reading *Playboy*.

Other explanations for the team's failure were:

1. The team's Moroccan chef poisoned the food for the *Seleção* in revenge for his country's 3-0 defeat.

2. Brazil were bribed to the tune of $20 million for each player. Ronaldo was against this (probably unimpressed by the amount) and for that reason he did not appear on the initial team-sheet. Then when he did play, he was so shocked he couldn't perform.

3. Suzana Werner, Ronaldo's fiancée, had been flirting with other men. This found some sympathy among the women in the office, who were generally of the opinion that no one would find Ronaldo's bald head sexy if they bumped into him on a suburban bus.

4. Suzana had given Ronaldo pills to calm him down on the day before the final. On the day of the final they discover that these might make him fail a drugs test, and Ronaldo gets horribly nervous as a result (despite the pills).

5. Ronaldo suffered an epileptic attack. Internazionale's team doctor denied this as strenuously as possible, with his own club's accusations against Ajax in the Nwankwo Kanu case very much in mind.

6. Ronaldo had failed a drug test after the Holland game. FIFA promised not to reveal this news on the condition that Brazil lost against France (a popular version in Holland, but not one that was taken very seriously in Brazil).

7. Brazil were crap. This outlandish theory was bravely offered by *Jornal do Brasil* journalist Armando Nogueira: "Brazil weren't obliged to win the final, but they were obliged to turn up. And it looked as though they had. So why did the final score read like a walk-over?"

Ronaldo himself probably got closest to the truth when he observed that all the excuses of the other players after the final were just trotted out to cover up their own failure.

Certainly it is not easy to play in the *Seleção*. Opinions tend to be extreme. Unless Brazil play fantastically well, they are inevitably accused of playing badly. Romário, for example, was highly critical during the match against Norway. "Brazil are terrible," he said. "They should bring on Edmundo." Edmundo did indeed come on, but after another ten minutes Romário pipes up again: "Edmundo is terrible, I think he should be substituted." Pelé, too, was highly critical, constantly proclaiming himself to be "worried". But then most people do not take Pelé very seriously. Asked by the enthusiastic Galvão Bueno of Globo TV during Brazil-Chile what marks he would give the team, Pelé replied: "During the first half I was worried, so a '4'. Second half, much better, a '6'. Overall though, a '7'."

After the final, the serious newspaper *Folha de São Paulo* published its World Cup XI. Not a single Brazilian was included. Most people, frustrated by Zagallo's impenetrable team selections, seemed to agree. Why did Bebeto play? Two old men I overheard in an ice-cream parlour claimed that *o chorão* (the cry-baby) was only in the team because of Antônio Carlos Magalhães, the president of the Senate and one of the most powerful people in Brazil, who wanted a player from his state, Bahia, up front. Others queried the non-selection of Denílson (popular with women, smiles a lot).

Another question on everyone's lips was: why was Roberto Carlos not substituted after ten minutes of every game? The arrogant left-back, continuously referred to on TV as "the second best player in the world", followed by a question mark left hanging in the air, is not popular in Brazil. Comments such as "I don't know how anybody can live on less than $20,000 a month" or "my watch is more expensive than most people's apartments" hardly endeared him to the Brazilian public. And nor was anyone impressed by his Winston Bogarde-style answer when asked why he was playing so poorly: "I can't be bothered about the opinions of the Brazilians. My family said I played well, why shouldn't I believe my family?"

Crucially, almost all the defenders were shaky. Whereas Brazil won in 1994 with an iron defence, this time around Junior Baiano was the symbol of all their fears. For 88 minutes he might be OK, but there were always two minutes of catastrophe around the corner, which led to Tore André Flo's goal for Norway, or Patrick Kluivert's for Holland. As if to explain his failures, one newspaper claimed the day after the squad returned that Junior Baiano is bisexual.

Cafú, who had played very convincingly, was injured before the Holland game, and gave way to the former melon seller Zé Carlos. Analogies were made with Djalma Santos, who came in for the 1958 final after an injury to the first-choice right back and became a hero. Nobody remembers the name of that right back. But after Brazil-Holland, everybody still remembered Cafú.

Given the fact that most of the team performed below expectations, the pressure mounted, above all, on Ronaldo. After the Norway game the squad were shown on TV enjoying a barbecue. One cartoon later portrayed Ronaldo smiling half-heartedly as he lifted on his fork a huge, dripping piece of meat in the shape of Brazil, saying: "Pretty heavy, huh?" Ronaldo's main problem was that the majority of Brazilians had never seen him play before the World Cup. Having left for Europe at a very young age, his fame had spread only after his exploits in Europe. In Brazil, European club games are broadcast almost exclusively on pay TV, to which most fans have no access, and of course the national team had played only friendlies in the run-up to France. So the public were expecting miracles from the Best Player on the Planet, and not surprisingly his efforts failed to satisfy them.

Some have even drawn the comparison with Raí, the brother of Socrates, who has always failed to reproduce his European club form for the national team. In the eyes of many, Ronaldo will not come of age until he can make them forget what Romário did for the *Seleção*. Until then he will remain "Ronaldinho" – little Ronaldo. That was the nickname he was given when he was in the 1994 World Cup squad along with another Ronaldo, who was fatter and older and therefore known as "Ronaldão" – big Ronaldo.

Ronaldo has said publicly that he does not find his nickname appropriate any more, but significantly "Ronaldinho" has stuck. Brazilians are unconvinced of his maturity, and it must be said that Ronaldo himself has done his utmost to confirm his boyish image. Television advertisements depict him still as the coke-sipping, crisp-eating, rabbit-toothed innocent, as opposed to the beer-gulping Romário, who has been through the school of hard knocks and isn't averse to stretching the rules if the situation demands it. Romário's last contribution to this World Cup was to put up a painting on the doors to the gents in his cafe showing Zagallo and Zico squatting on the toilet.

Yet however justified the criticism might have been, Brazil still had the capacity to play far better than most teams on earth. The problem was rather that this time there was a lack of conviction in the team that it was the best. As one of my colleagues at work put it: "In 1994, everybody knew we would win. This time, even when we won matches, we suffered all the time."

And football here, above all, is about pride – pride in being the best, the biggest, the most extreme in whatever. My colleagues asked me if the cities in Holland were decorated like the cities here for the World Cup – they wanted me to admit that there is no comparison between the two (which in fact there isn't). But they were genuinely shocked when I told them that my former firm did not close down for Holland's matches. My boss in Holland would probably just have said that he didn't like football. In Brazil you cannot say that you don't like *Copa do Mundo*.

back
HOME

I actually suspect that my boss in Brazil does not like football either, in the technical sense. He certainly doesn't talk about it. But he was still anxious to break up our business meeting 20 minutes before the start of the only Brazil game we watched at work. You have no choice. *Copa do Mundo* is not sport – it's carnival, it's a substitute for world politics ("Brazil must prevent France from entering the G7!"), it's you against me. Dutch people in Brazil had a hard time when Holland lost the semi-final. We were cruelly pestered at our jobs, on television, in cartoons. My Brazilian girlfriend rang from Switzerland the day after the game. "How do you feel?" she asked with a big smile (I could hear it). "I'm OK." "Are you sure?" she continued sadistically. "Well, I think that Holland should have won." "But then you lost!" End of discussion.

Benefiting from the football mania here, I dared to ask one of the partners if I could leave when Holland played Yugoslavia. He said (we're probably talking labour law here, or perhaps even human rights) that I had the same rights as anybody else in the office to watch my national team. At the risk of squandering my newly-acquired advantage, I pointed out that I then effectively had more rights than my colleagues, since I was also allowed to leave early for Brazil matches. But I was wrong: "When Brazil play," he replied, "you don't get early leave because of Brazil, but because the office closes."

For all the obsession with the *Seleção*, however, football nationalism in Brazil does not stop not entirely at the border. Many Brazilians also supported their *Irmãos Latinos* (Latin brothers), with the exception of Argentina. When Paraguay took France to the limits in extra-time of their second-round game I noticed that half the beach at Ipanema had wandered over to the pavement cafes and bars to lend their loud support to Paraguay's brave struggle.

Most Brazilians expected me as a Dutchman to do the same with the European teams, and were quite surprised to see on television the number of kids in France who were wearing Brazil shirts. I explained that most European countries have a somewhat different history which certainly does not make for brotherly feelings. They understood this in relation to Argentina of course. This was perfectly demonstrated in the bar of the Intercontinental hotel where we watched Holland beat Argentina. The Argentinian hotel guests, against a background of fireworks in celebration of their nation's defeat, started to shout at us: "Brasil! Brasil!" (meaning: Brazil will beat you in the semi-final). The Brazilian hotel guests replied with their own chant against the Argentinians: "Brasil! Brasil!" (meaning: "you hypocrites").

Nationalism, media bluff, promises, promises, promises. Despite everything, the regular fan turned out to be realistic and sometimes quite sarcastic about Brazil's efforts. Romário put this painfully into words when he described the selection of Ronaldo as Adidas Player of the Tournament as "an embarrassment for world football". *"O torcedor não é bobo,"* (the fan is not stupid) he added. Everybody could see that Ronaldo had not played his best and did not deserve the title.

And in contrast to the general disbelief in the media the day after the defeat, the reactions on the final day of all the Brazilians around me in the streets of Copacabana (decked out for the day with a yellow and green Eiffel Tower, and a huge stage on the beach for festivities afterwards) were astonishingly undemonstrative. Some had even stopped watching after the first half, with France leading 2-0. Others just shrugged and emptied their cans of Guaraná on the street. Nobody seemed desperate. Nobody threw themselves from one of the 12-storey buildings. Nobody said: "It's only a game." Everybody said: "Brazil were terrible."

One man could be seen in his fifth-floor window sticking his trumpet out from behind the curtains of his apartment and playing improvised tunes, continuing after the final whistle. The only excitement was caused by the rockets, which kids in the street, bored with the final result, started firing at each other. We did not know what to do, and ended up jumping on a bus that was half empty. Nobody cried. The bus was silent. It had rained all day and it kept on raining. Brazil had lost the World Cup. No day off that Monday.

a beautiful world

Patrick Mignon

In early 1997,

in Manchester, someone asked me: "So, how are the preparations for the World Cup coming along? Is the tension mounting?" It wasn't. In fact, at the time it was dead calm. Last Christmas a friend from London expressed his surprise that food manufacturers hadn't begun a huge promotional campaign for their products with the tournament looming. "The peas, for example, are really excellent in France," he said. Others were indeed making plans well in advance – my friend John had bet on a French victory months before.

But personally I didn't really feel anything much. As a sociologist, perhaps I shouldn't let emotion cloud my views too much anyway, but simply analyse things. And since Euro 96, like many others, I had frankly doubted the ability of the team to produce a style, on or off the pitch, that we could identify with. We are not like the English or Scottish, willing to dig in around the grounds right from the start of a campaign, with or without tickets, to support our national team.

French supporters need to feel that there's something in it for them. You may remember the French fans at Euro 96 – but more likely not. For although the team got to the semi-finals, the fans felt that they were offered very little.

In the run-up to France 98 there were plenty of additional factors which worked against any great upsurge of enthusiasm. There was the cost of the Stade de France and the impossibility of finding a team worthy of the name to play there, as well as a lot of fairly ugly manoeuvring by sponsors and the media. More significantly, perhaps, there was a complete failure on the part of the organisers to involve marginalised groups in the deprived suburban estates (*banlieues*) in any of the preliminaries. So for various reasons there was little sense of anticipation until shortly before June 10th.

And then, a month later, with the French team victorious, more than a million people were on the Champs Elysées, and all over France there were scenes of wild jubilation. It took me several days to return to reality, to get back into the swing of things after a month spent on a little cloud, and to digest the implications.

Did this outpouring of emotion disprove the theory that France's passion for football will always be limited? Or did it simply reflect the unique position occupied by the national side in French football culture compared with England, Spain or Italy, where the domination of the clubs sometimes works against the national team?

Certainly something unusual was going on. I remember talking to a Paris St Germain supporter a year before the tournament. Unlike the majority of serious fans, who were at that stage still wrapped up in their club and contemptuous of the national team, he was preparing seriously for the World Cup. He had taken over the management of a pizzeria in the southern suburbs of Paris, and was envisaging a "fantastic" scene during the finals, with tables outside and a big-screen television. My wife, a teacher in a secondary school in one of the toughest *banlieues*, told me her students had been completely uncontrollable during the draw for the first round groups. Visibly, for the young *black-blancs-beurs*, the children of migrants from France's colonies and of poor white families, things were hotting up. They weren't necessarily supporting France, but a kaleidoscope of T-shirts betrayed their identification with Zidane, with Brazil and Ronaldo, with Morocco, Tunisia and Cameroon. Even with Algeria, who hadn't qualified.

I was part of the committee charged with planning the treatment of fans during the tournament, with responsibility for making the police and other interested parties aware of the risk of hooliganism and of the difference between fans and hooligans. On the basis of such anecdotal evidence, I was able to tell them that I didn't expect an explosion of street violence during the competition. I wasn't wrong. True, there were some incidents on the Champs Elysées (after the sinister parade of giants the night before the tournament started), on the Canebière in Marseille, in Toulouse and in St Etienne, mostly sparked by the inhabitants of the *banlieues*. But these were almost all linked to the presence of a small number of English hooligans. In general, the initiatives developed for the tournament – giant screens, murals, football evenings in youth clubs and so on – had the desired effect.

As the event approached, I was increasingly happy and convinced it was going to be a success. There certainly was an anti-World Cup lobby, and since I had just had a book published (*The Passion of Football*), I inevitably got involved in a number of fairly angry arguments ("What's the problem if football is about stories of men, nations and violence?" "It's good that we can talk about the northern suburbs of Paris without going on about all their problems!" etc.) But driving home from work one day mulling over all this earnest polemic, it was suddenly brought home to me that it was little more than a distraction from the coming events. In the distance I could see a motorway bridge that links some waste ground to an industrial estate in one of the most isolated suburbs. As I got closer I was able to distinguish a blue flag with a white cross on it, and then some people who seemed to be very drunk, singing and wearing kilts...

In Paris, cafes began putting up flags of all the competing countries, signs appeared promising "Big screen here", pizza restaurants put up photos of the Italian squad, and everyone started to make their own little personal preparations: "Right, so for France-South Africa, you bring the wine, Sophie will make the dessert and I'll do the main course. We'll eat before the match and have the cake afterwards."

Even the negative news stories seemed only to encourage the sudden growth of this national sense of expectation. Tickets, for example. The condemnation of the French for being unable to organise a World Cup properly, in particular all the moralising from England or Holland, brought us closer together as a people. We ended up being almost proud of the Air France pilots' strike, showing our critics the world over how we could keep a cool head just days before the opening game. The feeling grew that this World Cup could be really good. I even started telling myself that the ubiquitous slogan *"C'est beau, un monde qui joue"* ("It's a beautiful world that plays") was a great one.

And, as it turned out, this World Cup was indeed beautiful, even taking into account the sometimes unpleasant reality of France and of football. It had all the nice surprises that you need to sustain the belief that football really is a game. Not necessarily great matches, but good matches, rarely ruined by the high stakes, a little spoilt by refereeing that was over fussy (ah, the superb first half of England-Argentina; oh, the sad second half) or just plain wrong (unluckily for Cameroon), but with a lot of great skill and technique and fair play, and some great goals. The extraordinary Japanese, like good school-children, had bought the shirts of all the French clubs to honour the host country. There were classics involving Cameroon, Nigeria, Brazil and Scotland. Away from the stadiums, the atmosphere in the tower blocks for Morocco's first match was electric. And in the streets and cafes something extraordinary was taking shape for France too.

But there were also the classics involving English and German hooligans. The former were exactly what we expected: I mark my territory, I drink on my territory, I hit whoever sets foot on my territory and I am helped by the opposing "fans", in this case the youths from the tough northern suburbs of Marseille and a few Olympique Marseille ultras who took the opportunity to make their mark on their own town centre.

For a short while it was the worst we could have imagined. But what can you do against individuals who might not shrink from killing people? The answer is to stay cool. For a moment I feared France would succumb to the siege mentality implicit in draconian anti-hooligan measures. But we managed to avoid that. True, the English fans in Lens had to watch the match through cafe windows or on small television sets, along with nervous CRS officers. But that was as far as it went.

The longer the tournament went on, the more the behaviour of the French fans helped to foster an atmosphere of festivity rather than aggression. But there again it took a bit of time. When France met Denmark in Lyon, any sense of occasion was limited to the station (the Scots were coming back from St Etienne), the Place Bellecourt (where the giant screen was) and on the road to the stadium. For the matches involving Morocco, Tunisia and Iran, by contrast, there was a fevered atmosphere in the districts where the majority of the inhabitants are north African. Otherwise everything was normal.

But then the suburbs began to descend on the town centres to watch the matches, and from France-Paraguay onwards things started to get very exciting. At St-Denis there were two World Cups. On one side there were those who had tickets, those who wore ties and followed the signs held by elegant hostesses bearing the names of the major sponsors, those who frequented the VIP villages. On the other side, all around them, there was something like a carnival, made up of people who didn't have tickets but just wanted to be there to savour the big-match atmosphere, eating sausages and chips and painting their faces, before going home to watch the match on television or settling down in front of one of the big screens.

The whole spectrum of people from the *banlieues* was to be found in front of those screens: diehard football people who had come in from the region's small clubs, blacks, whites, Arabs, both men and women, those who made the trip after congregating in the town square or their usual cafe, all surrounded by traders selling exotic sandwiches and T-shirts, events organised by anti-racist groups and young players from the four corners of the world who had come to take part in the "*Banlieue* World Cup" funded by the Ministry for Youth and Sport.

And things grew slowly. France-Paraguay: everyone had enough space to put their bottle down next to them. France-Italy: those who arrived late were a long way from the screen. France-Croatia: the roof of the disused factory that overlooked the area where the screen was situated was black with people. Below, the police hesitated, unsure whether or not to make people get down to avoid a catastrophe or leave them be (you can see the headline: **Factory Roof Collapses During Screening Of France-Croatia: X Dead**) They left them be. For France-Brazil, there was no more space by five o'clock in the afternoon and no more tiles visible on the factory roof.

Little by little, France came round to the World Cup, to the pleasure of football, and to the intensification of that pleasure that comes from getting behind your team. Of course, as a matter of duty, the government and other important political figures were supporting France. But apart from the transport minister Jean-Claude Gayssot or the leader of the Gaullist RPR party, Philippe Seguin, few could be considered real football lovers. However, Marie-George Buffet, minister for youth and sport who had previously declared her love for basketball, was converted. Prime Minister Lionel Jospin was even more impressive. During the presidential election campaign a few years earlier, he had sold himself as a skilled basketball player, with photos to prove it. And what would be more typical for France than a prime minister who has been to the top universities, but has never touched a football? But, with the miraculous love for the people that seized our leaders for these few weeks, he told us that in fact he was a goalkeeper! Proof that we hadn't been thinking about the World Cup in 1995.

There were more amazing revelations among the intellectuals: Alain Finkielkraut, Edgar Morin and other less well known characters stood up against those who followed the football-is-the-opium-of-the-masses theory. Instead, they sang the praises of a tournament that could get everyone out into the streets, bring people together, show how well France is integrated, eradicate the differences between men and women, and bring together the suburbs and the town centres – at least for a while.

These great figures paved the way for other highbrow academics (who would normally never go to matches and don't believe in competitive sport anyway) who were genuinely taken with the game. And such small conversions were the catalyst for many more. In fact, it was these newly-converted zealots who demanded punishment (insolvency, no doubt) for the only newspaper, *L'Equipe*, which continued to express any doubts about the team and its coach.

Support for France, however, was never unequivocal. In the first round we tended to support the small countries against the big ones. In the second we chose France, of course, but also Brazil and Nigeria. Even on the day of the final many of the young *beurs* were sporting Brazilian colours. But the game had captured the imagination of France, through the suspense of France-Paraguay and France-Italy, then through Lilian Thuram's two goals against Croatia. For many, the final was the icing on the cake. We had nothing against Brazil, in fact it was the dream final. But then came the glorious surprise. We won! Yes, France too can win the World Cup! We, too, can enjoy one of those liberating days when you shake hands or kiss people without knowing who they are, buy each other drinks, stay in the crowd out on the streets without fear, find common feelings with people we will never meet again. We were just elated that everything – nearly everything – had gone so well.

Afterwards, there was plenty of analysis of the events of July 12th. We talked, of course, about the victory for integration. The crowd in the streets of Paris was like the French side: black-white-arab and blue-white-red. With the tricolours flying we talked of a rediscovery of national pride, one which didn't automatically imply aggression or exclusion. We felt that victory in football was a symbol of a better self-image for France. We rejoiced in the new values embodied by Aimé Jacquet and his team: the work ethic in the absence of a creative genius, solidarity, discretion, modesty, awkwardness in communication – what we called "anti-Tapie values". And we beat the National Front. Or at least, if it wasn't a total defeat for Le Pen and his followers, it certainly gave them no pleasure whatsoever. They heard the *Marseillaise* sung by people who are, for them, foreigners. And that was a joy to behold.

Those who took part in these events, allowing themselves to become immersed in the peaceful crowds, lived an amazing experience. For many, it gave them a new perspective of themselves and of society as a whole. But that particularly applies to the immigration question and to those young French people who are the children of immigrants. The World Cup victory was a celebration of a multicultural France, but moreover that of an older idea of France, integrated and assimilated. Because this French team was not simply a representation of a relatively recent racial mixture, but also continued the tradition of French teams which, since the Thirties, have often been made up of players of Polish, Moroccan, Italian and Spanish origin.

Nevertheless, those Brazil shirts worn by so many young people from the *banlieues* should not be forgotten either. The post-final edition of *L'Express* carried one article celebrating the multi-coloured, festive crowds on the Champs Elysées and the integrating capability of the French team, but also one underlining the strong attraction of the National Front for the unqualified young people at the lower end of the social scale. There was a peaceful national unity in the celebrations of July 12th, but we know there is still a long way to go before the integration of white, black and north African youth can be considered a success.

What can we expect for the future of French football? Many young children will join clubs. Perhaps we will surpass last season's average First Division crowds of around 17,000. But it is not certain that we will see a huge increase. Because supporting France in the World Cup is a completely different experience – the French team belongs to everyone, even those who are not passionate about football. As for the clubs, many people are not ready to take up the habit where the territory still seems hostile.

Maybe we will see groups of young fans inspired by the events of July 12th. But the pro-National Front feelings that are present in many grounds will not disappear immediately, and spectators of Arab or African origin, under-represented in the majority of French grounds (but still slightly better than the one or two per cent present in English stadiums) won't suddenly be going to watch Paris St Germain or Racing Club Strasbourg. Equally, it's not certain that the increasing number of female fans noticed during the World Cup (more than 40 per cent of television viewers were women, and in the latter matches women certainly represented more than 20 per cent of spectators in the grounds) will be carried over into domestic games.

The realisation of the hopes expressed on the evening of July 12th, 1998 will depend on political responses to schooling, youth unemployment, the fight against racism and inner-city politics, but also to football. But even if those goals remain out of reach, the euphoria of July 12th should never become a bitter memory as a result – it was an experience worth savouring for its own sake.

Translated from the French by Richard Guy

CONTRIBUTORS

Anthony André lives a double life as a West Ham fan and the sports editor of Britain's biggest black weekly newspaper, the *Voice*.

Richard Augood fled the Fens at a creditably early age, and after a while spent studying computers in Leeds he married a Romanian. This gave him a valuable foot-up into the world of obscure football snobbery and he has never looked back.

Phil Ball works as a lecturer and educational consultant in the Basque country, where he has lived since 1991. He also worked in Oman and Peru after his football career peaked with a spell at North Ferriby reserves. He has supported Grimsby Town from birth and has contributed to *When Saturday Comes* since 1987.

Ivan Briscoe is 28 years old and adrift in Argentina, working as a reporter on the English-language paper the *Buenos Aires Herald*. When not avoiding tango classes, he finds time to appreciate the flowing game of River Plate and the disaster area of Racing Football Club, even if his heart still lies broken in Maine Road.

Mark Brownlow, 30, swapped Wiltshire for Vienna and now works as a translator, English teacher, Internet publisher and freelance journalist. Fortunately, his Austrian wife has a proper job. His love of football began after he lost a bet with his dad on the outcome of the 1977 FA Cup final.

Adriaan Grijns works as a lawyer in Rio de Janeiro. He is very happy that his relationship with his Brazilian girlfriend survived the summer thanks to Ronald de Boer missing his penalty, just as he felt utterly relieved in 1994 when Branco destroyed Holland's World Cup hopes.

Roberto Gotta is 34 and lives in Bologna. He works mainly as a basketball journalist, but his first love is football, to which he became emotionally attached at the age of four when his father took him to see Bologna play Roma. He discovered English football in 1974, while watching the FA Cup final. Since then, he has cared much more about Fulham or Newcastle than Bologna or Vicenza.

Uli Hesse-Lichtenberger wasted half his adult life going to university and playing in punk bands, before becoming a freelance sports writer. He has contributed to numerous magazines in Germany, England and Israel, but is happy to say that he has never watched a football match from the press box. He is married with an eight-year-old son and lives in Witten, which is handy for travelling to watch Borussia Dortmund.

Dave Hill is a journalist and the author of *Out Of His Skin*, about John Barnes and Liverpool, and *England's Glory*, about the 1966 World Cup. He once had trials for Bristol City, but is now restricted to the role of creaking libero in kickabouts with his two young sons and their schoolmates.

Andrew Jackson is 52. He maintains a residual hatred of Woking despite the fact that the team he grew up supporting, Guildford City, is now defunct. He subsequently picked up a deep affection for Nottingham Forest, whom he follows wistfully from the Baltic island of Bornholm, where he is a teacher.

Jeremy Lennard was born in Birmingham in 1964. He has worked as a teacher and freelance journalist in the Middle East and Portugal, but now lives and works in Bogotá. He writes on Colombia for many publications, including the *Guardian* and the *Economist*.

Justin McCurry is a staff writer at the English-language newspaper the *Daily Yomiuri*. His lifelong support for Wolverhampton Wanderers was ideal preparation for the disappointment of Japan's World Cup debut. He lives in the western port city of Osaka – a bit like Liverpool minus the footballing tradition – with his wife and daughter.

Robin McMillan grew up as a Raith Rovers fan in Fife, but has lived in New York since 1979. Once a reporter on the *Fife Free Press*, he is now a magazine editor specialising in sport, and has written or co-written four books. He was the editor-in-chief of Sports Publishing Group, who produced the official programmes for the 1994 World Cup.

Mark McQuinn was born in Stockport but got out quickly and has never lived in any one place for more than four years since. He jinxes the local football team in just about every place he moves to and has seen seven relegated so far. He currently teaches at the School of Oriental and African Studies in London.

Patrick Mignon is 47. He discovered football through Raymond Kopa, the 1958 World Cup and Stade Reims and continued to read *L'Equipe* secretly throughout the Seventies while studying history and sociology. He now writes and lectures on the sociology of sport at the Institut National des Sports et de l'Education Physique in Paris.

Mike Mitchell was born in Liverpool and is a third-generation Koppite. Since leaving Merseyside in search of gainful employment he has led an itinerant existence in Mexico, Brazil and the United States. He lives in Mexico City and works a journalist.

Osasu Obayiuwana is a qualified solicitor from Nigeria, but for the past ten years he has been a print and radio journalist covering African football from his base in London.

Gary Oliver is a regular contributor to *When Saturday Comes*, *The Absolute Game* and the Raith Rovers fanzine *Stark's Bark*. His birth in Kirkcaldy during season 1962-63 coincided with Raith being relegated, gaining only nine points from 34 matches. However, he insists the two events were unconnected. He now lives in Musselburgh and hopes never to meet Ally McCoist.

Norbert N. Ouendji is the deputy editor and sports editor of *Le Messager* newspaper in Cameroon and also works as a freelance writer. Brought up in the west of the country, he now lives in Yaoundé.

Renato Pandza is a 28-year-old journalist with the daily newspaper *Slobodna Dalmacija*. Although Zagreb is his home town, he is a diehard fan of Hajduk Split and was a founder of their supporters' magazine in 1996. He is definitely not prejudiced by that fact – in fact many of his best friends are Dinamo Zagreb fans.

John Perlman presents *AM Live*, a current affairs programme on South African national radio, and is a football commentator for the South African Broadcasting Corporation.

Dragomir Pop-Mitic is a lawyer by trade but now works for an import-export firm when he's not following the fortunes of Partizan Belgrade. He is 36.

David Roberts was born in Zimbabwe, brought up in Britain and now lives in Santiago. He is the editor of the English-language *News Review*, which tends to relegate match reports to the small print on the results page whenever Middlesbrough lose.

Rutger Slagter is a 27-year-old freelance journalist, who studied US history before specialising in Dutch football. He used to marshall the defence for ASC Oegstgeest, before moving on to play for Ajax (at cricket).

Knut Are Tvedt is, among other things, sports editor of *Aschehoug & Gyldenals Store Norske Leksikon*, the Norwegian equivalent of *Encyclopedia Britannica*.

BOOKS

WSC Books is a publishing imprint
created by the monthly independent
magazine *When Saturday Comes*, with the
aim of providing a platform for original
and innovative writing on football.
Back Home is the first new title to appear
under the imprint.

We aim to publish a small number of
quality titles each year, which will address
topics outside the mainstream (including
football in other countries) in an intelligent
and accessible manner. And that means no
hooligan diaries.

We welcome ideas for book projects and
draft manuscripts (please include an SAE).

WSC Books
9 Whitehall Park
London
N19 3TS

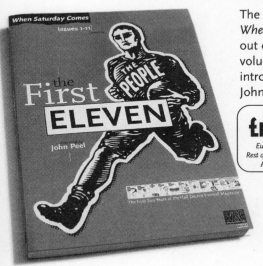

WSC
When Saturday Comes

MAGAZINE & SUBSCRIPTION DETAILS

When Saturday Comes is an independent monthly magazine focusing on all aspects of football culture from the fans' perspective. The magazine was started in 1986, a time when Luton Town were a force in the land and cabinet ministers were considerably less eager to identify themselves as football fans than they are now. *WSC* continues to produce critical football writing with a sense of humour. Look out for it underneath the pile of glossy football mags at your newsagents. Or, to be sure of securing a copy of the latest issue, visit Sportspages bookshop in London or Manchester.

Alternatively, take out a subscription to *WSC* and have your copy delivered to your door before it is in the shops. You'll be guaranteed the next 12 months of the best in independent football writing, plus any *WSC* supplements and freebies, all at an inflation-proof rate.

1 year subscription
£25.40 UK
Europe £32
Rest of World £39

To order: Send your name, address, a cheque payable to *When Saturday Comes*, or your Visa/Mastercard details to:

***When Saturday Comes*, FREEPOST KE8091, London EC1B 1SA (No Stamp Needed in UK*)**

OR: CALL 24HR MASTERCARD/VISA LINE 0171 490 0800 FAX 0171 490 1598

If you are paying by credit card please enclose your credit card name, number, expiry date, and statement address if it is different to the one you wish your books to be delivered to. ***Overseas send to:** *WSC*, 2 Pear Tree Court London EC1R 0DS United Kingdom